THE

MINISTRY

OF THE

UNVEILED

FACE

ENDORSEMENTS

Sometimes an angel comes to show the way when we need it most. *The Ministry of the Unveiled Face* brings an angel's gentleness, wisdom, and serene conviction, as Janet Fichter shows us the path to deeper relatedness with God. When we ponder growing in faith, we usually mean living before God with greater authenticity. This is Mrs. Fichter's invitation. Because she is such an authentic Christian, her offer resounds with authority. To go deeper with God, for genuine transformation as Christ's followers, we shed our masks to open our imperfect selves to God's gentle, dynamic grace. Janet Fichter ushers the reader who dares transparency to such a place, a relationship both exciting and fearful. And what are the fruits of this transformation? An invigorated witness that is as loving as it is true, as free of fear as it is bold. Walk with Janet down this path of Christ's light and grace.

THE REVEREND DALE ROSENBERGER

Minister and Author

What a beautiful and profound book, yet simple to understand and apply in daily life. Through her stories and guidance, Janet Fichter has crafted a handy tool for us as we seek to honor the Lord of our souls, who only asks us to do what He did, and promises that we'll do even more as we advance His kingdom on earth. Are you, with unveiled face, reconciling your friends and God? Will you be the catalyst that brings people into intimate relationship with their Savior? Do you, like me, struggle to understand how to present Jesus? Do you fear rejection or do you lack confidence because you think you don't know enough? This book will rest those fears and give you encouragement to move forward in your own ministry of the unveiled face.

CHRIS TRACY

Writing Coach and Author, Founder of Beautiful Word

I was thoroughly swept away by this remarkable book. I found myself reading entire chapters out loud to my wife because I was so compelled to share the treasures hidden in its pages. *The Ministry of the Unveiled Face* invites you into an intimate relationship with Christ and reveals the deep calling to allow Christ to live through you, revealing His beauty and goodness to a world in desperate need of light and life. Janet Fichter's book provides you with practical tools, and challenges you to be more than a reader. No matter who you are and where you are in life, YOU are a minister, unveiling God's goodness to others as you step out in faith to the leading of Christ.

JAN EITEL

Pastor and Founder of Hearts for the World International Ministries

WE ARE TO BE THE UNVEILED FACE THAT REVEALS
THE GOODNESS AND GLORY OF CHRIST

THE
MINISTRY
OF THE
UNVEILED
FACE

JANET E. FICHTER

Ambassador International
GREENVILLE, SOUTH CAROLINA & BELFAST, NORTHERN IRELAND
www.ambassador-international.com

The Ministry of the Unveiled Face

©2022 by Janet E. Fichter
All rights reserved.

ISBN: 978-1-64960-200-8
eISBN: 978-1-64960-264-0

Cover Design by Hannah Linder Designs
Interior Typesetting by Dentelle Design
Edited by Avrie Roberts

AMBASSADOR INTERNATIONAL
Emerald House
411 University Ridge, Suite B14
Greenville, SC 29601
United States
www.ambassador-international.com

AMBASSADOR BOOKS
The Mount
2 Woodstock Link
Belfast, BT6 8DD
Northern Ireland, United Kingdom
www.ambassadormedia.co.uk

The colophon is a trademark of Ambassador, a Christian publishing company.

To the Great I AM

Who Beckons Entrance to the Realm Behind the Veil

God of Glory's Goodness

Radiance of Joy, Brilliance of Love

Author of Truth's Word

Master Gardener, Relentless Sower, Architect of Creation

Fragrance of Life,

I Thank You.

Open my heart that I respond

With goodness, like You, Holy One.

Who loves each one, no limits spoken.

Healer of all hearts, once broken.

May I, like You, walk with each soul,

Unveiling truth, that they'd be whole.

Janet Fischer, *Unveiled* poem

"And we all, with unveiled face, beholding as in a mirror the glory of the Lord,
are being transformed into the same image from glory to glory,
just as from the Lord, the Spirit."

2 Corinthians 3:18 (NASB1995)

TABLE OF CONTENTS

ACKNOWLEDGMENTS

Like the construction of a bridge, the culmination of the message given in *The Ministry of the Unveiled Face* involved many builders. I wish to thank and acknowledge those who helped guide the construction here, apologetic to any I've missed.

- To my sister, Lucy M. Floyd, who spoke the words of truth that unveiled my own blind eyes, and who championed me along each step of this writing journey. Her guidance and deep knowledge of Scripture were anchors.

- To my mother, Margaret Hooper, whose lifelong prayers continue to transcend time and space and still lay before God's throne of grace.

- To my husband, Elmar Fichter, whose patience, support, and generosity came alongside me to cycle up the hill yet again. Thank you for always being my "steady."

- To those who ensured no component of construction was missed as this bridge was built: Chris Tracy (writing coach, author, founder of Beautiful Word), Elizabeth Garrett (editor, coach, and author, Polish Point Editing), the welcoming and helpful staff at Ambassador International (Dr. Sam Lowry, Avrie Roberts, Anna Riebe Raats, Mark Linton, Chris Jackson, Susanna Maurer, Katie Cruice Smith, Daphne Self, and Bethany McDaris).

- To those daily unveiling Christ's goodness to others in their lives and ministry, and who took the time to support me in mine: Diane

M. Campbell (friend and author), the Reverend Dale Rosenberger (Minister and Author), Jan Eitel (Pastor and Founder of Hearts for the World International Ministries), Kathy Robinson (cherished sister and partner in crime), and Mark Hooper (beloved brother and role model).

- To precious friends and cheerleaders: Susanna Romanek, Sue Janssen, Terry Halladay, Toni Bower, Kay Shafer, Cheryl Velk, Debi Curtis, Nancee Schroeder and members of Writers on the Rock.

- To the stalwarts of our faith, who inspired clarity regarding the brilliance that lies behind the veil and the simplicity of the priesthood of all believers: Oswald Chambers, Dutch Sheets, Charles Spurgeon, E. M. Bounds, Billy Graham, and countless others.

INTRODUCTION

The Great Commission of Jesus directed His disciples to go into all the world and preach the good news (Matthew 28:19). Followers of Christ should be inspired to help others come to know Him. However, the call to "evangelize" often conjures up undesirable images of walking inner city streets with a megaphone yelling for nameless hordes of people to repent. Christians are hesitant in their witness for Christ because no one relishes the idea of facing opposition, ridicule, or persecution—all potential reactions in current society. But Scripture clearly says we are called to share the gospel message. In truth, it isn't that difficult. When we consider witnessing as simply helping others understand Christ's goodness, we realize it is a profound honor.

This book, *The Ministry of the Unveiled Face*, presents evangelism through a fresh perspective, emphasizing the principle that our words, acts of compassion, and prayers reveal Jesus to others. Realizing unbelievers cannot see into the spiritual realm, our motivation to interaction with them is ignited by love and a genuine desire to help deepen their understanding. With an invisible veil, Satan has blinded the spiritual vision of those who haven't yielded their lives to Christ. But believers are given the amazing privilege of seeing beyond the veil into the spiritual realm of God's kingdom. Strengthened by this privilege, we abandon our human hesitancies and embrace Christ's heart of compassion for all.

The anchor verse for this study is 2 Corinthians 3:18:

> "And we all, with unveiled face, beholding the glory of the Lord, are being transformed into the same image from one degree of glory to another. For this comes from the Lord who is the Spirit."

Imagine a veil hanging in front of you, blocking your vision. A gift of amazing value and beauty exists behind it, but you are prohibited from seeing it. Somehow a friend of yours is able to view the gift, for there is no veil blocking his or her sight. If your friend has learned how to remove the veil, wouldn't you want them to help you also view what lies behind it?

Now imagine yourself as the friend who *is* able to see the priceless gift on the other side of the covering. You have been given the privilege of sight, but this ability brings the opportunity of assisting others to also see. Wouldn't you embrace the honor of helping them get rid of the shield that blocks the gift behind it?

We are the unveiled face revealing Christ's goodness to a hurting and confused world. Because Christ is in us, His presence is unveiled to whomever we interact with. In our faithful sharing of God's love and truth, the light of Christ penetrates the realms of darkness, opening blind eyes and softening hardened hearts.

The Ministry of the Unveiled Face is for all who yearn to know their purpose in Christ, who long for greater faithfulness and devotion, and who seek clarity for their specific calling. Grounding our evangelistic perspective in the purity of the call to help others understand God's goodness simplifies our purpose. Our fears and resistance melt away, and we embrace the great privilege of sharing Jesus's love.

CHRIST UNVEILED UNDER THE NEW COVENANT

This witness is what the Apostle Paul addresses in the anchor verse referenced above (2 Corinthians 3:18). Throughout this chapter in 2

Corinthians, Paul contrasts the Old and New Covenants. He intended for the Corinthians (and for us) to understand how the New Covenant of faith in Christ brings a revelation of God's glory that was impossible under the Old Covenant. Paul recounts how the Old Covenant required the presence of the Lord to be shielded from humanity because its brilliance was too powerful an encounter.

Paul then labels the Old Covenant as transitory and focuses on rejoicing in the New Covenant gift: direct access to God through Christ. Those who have accepted Jesus as their Lord and Savior come face to face with God's glory as they are transformed into the very image of His goodness by the power of the Holy Spirit.

Many people do not understand the Jewish laws of the Old Covenant, nor can they fathom how Jesus provided a New Covenant which transformed humanity's access to the Most High God (see Chapter Six for detailed explanation). Eyes closed to the indescribable goodness of Jesus Christ can only be opened through yielding one's heart and life to Christ. The essence of this ministry is that our daily witness, unveiled face to veiled face, gives sight to the blind and reveals the glory behind the veil.

Simplicity finds its home in this ministry, where persevering prayers and expressed words of truth (based on Scripture) bring an "unveiling" of God's goodness and sovereign glory. Responding to Jesus's voice in our interactions with others brings sweet fellowship with Christ as we walk out our faith. We cannot deny that the god of this age has spiritually blinded people, but speaking the gospel's good news and confronting the realms of darkness with prayer brings revelation to hindered sight.

To live out this call, we move forward step by step as we listen for God's voice and obey His leading. If we willingly respond to the open doors and opportunities God provides, the Holy Spirit does the work. In faith, we trust our Sovereign Lord to heal and transform the hearts and minds of those coming to know Him.

A MINISTRY BATHED IN PRAYER

Since prayer is foundational to ministry, each chapter ends with a prayer. Like an invigorating walk on a brisk spring morning, interceding for others envelops and empowers those living out the ministry of the unveiled face. Intercession confronts the schemes of evil, moves the mountains of resistance, and precedes the soul's transformation. The prayers offered are ones I pray regularly. I hope the examples bless you as God unveils His goodness in and through you.

REFLECTIONS AS THE STUDY BEGINS

1. Consider your own hesitancy in sharing Christ. What anxieties does the call to witness bring you?

_____

_____

_____

2. How do you personally interpret the Great Commission given in Matthew 28:19? What does "going into all the world" look like for you?

_____

_____

_____

3. Explain your background and understanding of the Old and New Covenants. How do you envision the spiritual realm that lies behind the veil in light of the fact that we now live under the New Covenant?

_____

_____

_____

4. As you begin this study, consider what you hope to take away. In what areas are you seeking direction? What do you wish to learn?

_____

_____

_____

Deeper insight into the principles of unveiling the gift of Christ's goodness to others comes from further examination of the veil itself. The analogy of Christ as our bridegroom helps set the purpose for why we must work diligently to help others remove the veil shielding spiritual understanding. Chapter One explores this marriage metaphor.

CHAPTER ONE

THE BRIDEGROOM'S UNVEILING

"Behold, you are beautiful, my love, behold, you are beautiful!
Your eyes are doves behind your veil."

Song of Solomon 4:1a

David could not take his eyes off Lauren as she gracefully walked down the aisle of the sanctuary. How he longed to see her face, now shadowed by a delicate lace veil. He knew her beauty, of course. But he couldn't control the short, quick breaths betraying his nervous energy. He yearned to gaze at the sparkling eyes and beautiful smile of his soon-to-be bride.

Because the imagery of removing the wedding veil was important to them, they chose a more traditional ceremony. David's removal of the delicate lace veil would provide a lifelong reminder of the moment they committed to cherish each other forever. The ceremony progressed, his anticipation causing him to fidget. His best man gently nudged him hoping it would stop the weight-shifting. Finally, the minister provided the long-awaited permission, "You may kiss your bride." David lifted the veil, and the longed-for intimacy enhanced by this symbolic act became the first step in their new life together.

Traditional weddings include this cherished ritual of unveiling the bride's face. In an instant, unity is birthed. The husband and wife walk hand in hand into an unknown future, knowing they will share good times, endure hardship, and hold fast to each other day by day.

THE SYMBOLISM OF THE VEIL

The symbolism of this marital "unveiling" applies to one's relationship with Jesus Christ as well. A spiritual unveiling occurs when a person yields their life to Him. In that moment of surrender, the bridegroom reveals His goodness and steadfast love for the bride. This unearthly unity transcends anything imaginable in the natural realm.

In the spiritual realm, the veil symbolizes an unseen covering that prevents a person from receiving and understanding the Kingdom of God. Like the bride's veil, this supernatural covering is removed when a relationship with Christ begins. With the absence of the veil comes illumination and transformation as Jesus molds and makes us more like Him. We live our lives in awe of and in devotion to the One who loves us eternally. With transformed hearts, mindsets change. A new, heavenly perspective reigns over natural inclinations, and our sinful nature is exchanged for one with faith as its foundation. Like the husband and wife, we commit to trust and sacrifice for our cherished love, Jesus Christ, and His undying devotion protects us and provides for us eternally.

THE BRIDEGROOM'S LOVE

In the Old Testament book, Song of Solomon, God's love for His church is portrayed poetically, comparing it to the tender love of marriage. Reading Song of Solomon 2:10-14 is like listening in on the bride describing the voice of the bridegroom calling to her:

> "Arise, my love, my beautiful one, and come away, for behold, the winter is past; the rain is over and gone. The flowers appear on the earth, the time of singing has come, and the voice of the turtledove is heard in our land. The fig tree ripens its figs, and the vines are in blossom; they give forth fragrance. Arise, my love,

my beautiful one, and come away. O my dove, in the clefts of the rock, in the crannies of the cliff, let me see your face, let me hear your voice, for your voice is sweet, and your face is lovely."

The analogy is purposeful, for God calls everyone to this same intimacy and union. He invites us to come to a place where growth and fruit are abundant. There in the protected cleft of the rock the bridegroom holds his beloved's face. This picture symbolizes the love Christ has for all who yield to His call. His voice invites us to a place of refuge and a relationship that acknowledges vulnerability.

Greater depth to the comparison comes with the realization that not only is the bride's innocence and beauty a joy to the bridegroom, but the illumination of the bridegroom's goodness brings an unimaginable peace and security to the bride. Is it any wonder, then, why the Apostle Paul addresses the removal of the veil as a transformative moment when the Lord imparts His glory to the soul of the one who receives Him (2 Corinthians 3:18)?

Below is a prayer of gratitude I encourage you to pray as you begin reading this book. I sincerely hope you will be enlightened and unburdened, for we serve a good and compassionate bridegroom who cherishes us like no other.

PRAYER

Thank You, Jesus, for Your unfathomable love. Thank You for hiding me in the cleft of the rock and for removing the veil that shields Your goodness. Thank You for making a way for me to be transformed, from glory to glory, as we walk together in unity. Use me, Lord, to bring about the unveiling of Your goodness to others. I trust You to bring open doors and opportunities for me to minister to others in your name. Amen.

REFLECTIONS ON
CHAPTER ONE

1. Are you able to view your walk with Christ as the intimate journey described in Song of Solomon? Explain any struggles you may have with this picture. For example, does it make you feel too vulnerable?

_____

_____

_____

2. Expound upon how the analogy of Christ as our bridegroom comforts you:

_____

_____

_____

3. In considering your walk with Christ, how might your faith and trust in the bridegroom grow by envisioning a unity so personal? Does it help you more vividly visualize Christ beside you?

_____

_____

_____

4. Are you able to trust in the complete goodness of Christ or are there areas in which you doubt His love? Because Jesus understands the human condition (Hebrews 4:15) we may subconsciously attribute human characteristics to Him, preventing us from embracing the sovereign nature of our Lord's goodness. In what ways might you yearn for greater understanding of Christ's goodness?

_____

_____

_____

The intimacy we have with Jesus, our bridegroom, encompasses a tender and eternal friendship. In the following chapters, you will read personal anecdotes illustrating the ministry of the unveiled face where I share experiences from cherished relationships. Chapter Two highlights moments where others (including myself) discovered how precious it is to have a friendship with Jesus.

LET ME INTRODUCE YOU TO A FRIEND OF MINE

"A man who has friends must himself be friendly,
but there is a friend who sticks closer than a brother."

Proverbs 18:24 (NKJV)

As we walk out each day of our lives in fellowship with Christ, we come to know the depths of His love for us and learn to trust Him unequivocally. Jesus calls us friends, after all (John 15:15), so the relationship we have with Him is—in large part—of a trusted companion. When we introduce our own friends and loved ones to Christ, we invite them to that same bond.

Years ago, I became close friends with a colleague from work, Jean. I was a young woman in a troubled marriage. Jean was a busy mother with a toddler at her heels, managing a household and holding down a full-time job. Despite her more hectic schedule, Jean responded to God's prompting and introduced me to another friend of hers, Susanna. Jean made sure we met, and in no time at all, Susanna and I became the very best of friends. How grateful I am to Jean for connecting us. She knew Susanna and I would have a lot in common and be a support for each other. Even now, after thirty years, Susanna and I continue to pray together, providing counsel for life's challenging times and rejoicing in joyful seasons.

Like Jean did for me, it can be a social norm to connect people we believe will spiritually support one another, trusting they will speak words of truth and encouragement into the other person's life. So, why are we so hesitant to introduce our non-Christian friends to Jesus, the very best friend of all? We worry needlessly about offending them or potentially jeopardizing the relationship. If you think about it, however, once they know Jesus, any initial offense will surely vanish. The Bible tells us Jesus is the "friend who sticks closer than a brother" (Proverbs 18:24), and we can't go wrong taking time to guide our friends to seek a relationship with Him. In our hearts we know there will never be a better companion than Jesus.

A UNIQUE FRIENDSHIP

Obviously, there are many distinctions between a friendship with Jesus and a friendship with another human being. But it is a joy and privilege to help others know they can have a personal relationship with Creator God, through His son, Jesus Christ. We who have had the veil removed from our own spiritual eyes prayerfully respond to the call of unveiling Christ's goodness to others. The progression of unveiling is a mystery we never fully grasp, although we trust in the freedom that comes as God reveals the intricacies of His character.

When we speak words of hope and truth into the lives of others, does the veil rip just a bit, or is it completely torn apart? The answer to that question lies in the Holy Spirit's sovereign power. In 2 Corinthians 3:18, the Apostle Paul speaks of the transformation as moving from "one degree of glory to another," noting we *are being* transformed. This tells us a process is involved. Understanding the intricacies of the journey takes time, and insight comes along the way. In joyous faith we enter into the process of God's work in the lives of others because we are the bridegroom's friends. We lay the steps of transformation at His feet while we focus on the immediate opportunity—to act in love, speak words of truth, and pray with a dogged determination for the revelation of Christ to take hold.

Sadly, I can count on one hand the number of people I have actually prayed the prayer of salvation with. I say this to make clear I am not an evangelist, and I struggle with hesitations, fears, and insecurities when it comes to sharing Christ with others. Being an introvert, the eagerness to interact with others rarely sprints to the forefront of my desires. But Christ calls me to share, and by His grace and strength I am equipped to do so.

When I think about how Jesus chose me to be His friend, it makes me more eager to introduce others to Him. Reflection on Christ's love for me helps me identify with His heart of compassion for the person I'm reaching out to. God grants plenty of opportunities to be a witness of His goodness. Often I respond with a questioning plea for help; but other times, His prompting is clear and I share His truth with confidence. With every open door, I trust veils are torn and spiritual revelation occurs.

THE VEIL REMOVED (MY STORY)

It may be helpful to read a few of my experiences, including the time Christ was unveiled and became my Lord and Savior. Throughout my life, I've been very close with my siblings (two sisters and one brother). My oldest sister, Lucy, took the time to explain God's plan of redemption to my sister, Kathy, and me many years ago. Even though my family and I went to church every Sunday, I didn't have a personal relationship with Jesus. We attended a mainline Methodist church which elevated Jesus as an example of God's goodness, but not God incarnate.

As a child, I didn't comprehend that God sent Jesus to die in my place and receive the punishment I deserved for my sins. I didn't know He could be my closest friend either, because the veil still covered my spiritual eyes. Lucy babysat for a family from that same Methodist church, who took the time to explain salvation to her. Sadly, the church later asked this family to leave for proselytizing such "radical" ideas. Once Lucy walked Kathy and me through certain Bible verses, we were eager to take the next steps to know Jesus personally. A cherished childhood memory is of talking and praying into the late hours of the night with Kathy in the bedroom she and I shared.

After I prayed the prayer of salvation, God began unveiling His truths and goodness. I was twelve years old at the time and immediately began sharing this blessed revelation with my friends. Junior high school didn't deter me much, for I had the innocence and purity of a newfound faith in Jesus. Peer pressure to conform was strong, and others often made fun of me for trying to share Christ's love.

One day at lunch, I noticed a seventh-grade girl, Rosemary, far more an outcast than I. She was overweight and unkempt—an easy target for being ostracized and bullied. Rosemary sat by herself on the steps near the cafeteria door while another group of students sat off to the side. I responded to God's prompting by sitting beside her and telling her how much Jesus loved her. She looked up and smiled shyly. A simple conversation followed, and I believe my words about Christ's love touched her spirit and tore a bit of the veil away, laying groundwork for God's goodness to be made known.

Another girl nearby overheard and immediately shared with her friends what I said. The crowd broke out in accusing laughter. I never regretted telling Rosemary about Christ and how He loved her. And while I have no idea how her life turned out, I trust the truth I spoke made an impact in penetrating the veil which shielded her spiritual vision.

That same year, I organized a Bible study during lunchtime with a few friends, one of whom is now a minister. Later in high school, I hosted a weekly evening Bible study at my house for some friends. I was an amateur and often spoke impulsively, my witness far from perfect. But I sincerely wanted to introduce my friends to the very best friend of all. They knew faith was foundational to my life and I trust our discussions helped them consider exploring a personal relationship with Jesus. I am still in touch with many of these same friends who are now raising families in the life of faith. I believe an opening in the veil occurred for God to take the next steps of revelation. I simply planted and watered seeds.

MY FATHER MEETS MY FATHER

In those years, my father never fully understood faith was based on an individual relationship with Jesus. Personal salvation was not a tenet of the Methodist church he attended, and he thought our newfound belief system was cultish. As a result, we prayed diligently, but treaded cautiously in any attempt to present the gospel to him. Fast forward to my adult years, when my father had a massive stroke. Though he lived for thirteen years as a stroke victim, at the time we had no idea how long he might survive.

I visited my parents regularly after the stroke, and one day God prompted me to give Dad an opportunity to pray the prayer of salvation. I shared a few Scriptures with him and talked about God's plan for redemption in Christ. I asked if he'd ever prayed to accept Jesus as Lord and he admitted he hadn't. Since the stroke severely affected his speech, we prayed together with him repeating my words as best he could. At seventy-four, the veil that covered his spiritual vision for so many years tore, and the journey to know Christ began. My brother, Mark, discipled him, regularly praying and reading God's Word together. It took courage to witness so directly to the man who had been such a powerful head of our household, but the time was God-ordained. It was the right moment to introduce my father to my Father.

TRUSTING GOD'S SOVEREIGN GUIDANCE

These stories relay times I clearly heard and obeyed God's prompting to introduce others to Jesus, the friend who sticks closer than a brother. Sadly, there are far more examples when fear engulfed me and I did not respond to the urging of the Holy Spirit. I have learned over the years that if we are unclear, we mustn't wrestle with doubt to the point of frustration wondering, *Should I say this? Should I do this? What will happen if . . . ?* More likely, God wants us to interact with those He brings our way. When uncertainty surfaces, we pray to Jesus, our friend. He will correct our mistakes and help us rest in the confident assurance of God's sovereign intervention. Any interaction with Christ's love as its foundation will be blessed.

And any interaction bathed in prayer will be effective. In Paul's letter to the Ephesians, he prayed they would have "the Spirit of wisdom and of revelation in the knowledge of him" (Ephesians 1:17). In every encounter we have with those who don't know Christ, we can pray this same way. Since we are seated in the heavenly places with Christ (Ephesians 2:6), we can be confident God will bring the revelation of Christ to our friends and loved ones. When we pray, our words are used to remove the veil clouding their spiritual vision (note: Chapter Seven explores the role of prayer in greater depth). With the Psalmist, we desire for our friends to experience the brilliance of revelation.

"Those who look to him are radiant,
and their faces shall never be ashamed."

Psalm 34:5

A FRIENDSHIP OF AWE AND WONDER

Though *wondrous* and *immeasurable* describe God's attributes, knowing His love for us as a friend brings a sense of safety to the troubled soul. Trusting the sincerity of this friendship opens the door to discovering more and more about the unfathomable traits of our Creator. Of course, we don't assume that a callous familiarity defines the relationship. Rather, we acknowledge the great I AM exists in ways our limited understanding cannot grasp (Exodus 3:14; John 8:58). That means, while God is intimately acquainted with the uniqueness of every individual, His Spirit transcends through all realms of our being (Psalm 139) creating awe that can overwhelm.

This dichotomy is difficult to grasp for those who've never yielded their soul to Him. The intricate beauty of the relationship is that God imparts these mysteries at just the right times, when He knows we are ready to receive a greater understanding (Psalm 25:14; Jeremiah 33:3). In our wonder at His majesty, we leave the work of revelation in the hands of our Sovereign Lord.

Perhaps God is laying on your heart a need to introduce a loved one to Jesus. Your prayers for them will bring new spiritual insight. Along those lines, I've included a prayer you can pray specifically for that person. May God's word of truth go forth and take root into the depths of their souls as the unveiling begins.

PRAYER

Lord God, I pray for _____. I ask You to send forth all the forces of Heaven—the angels and archangels and the powers of truth and light—to bring messages and messengers to inspire and confront, to guide and direct, to comfort and heal. May your truth and love cast out all fear and break bondages. Remove the veil shielding your glory. Instill in _____ a hunger and thirst for righteousness and an awareness of sin. Bind up a spirit of pride and grant _____ a godly sorrow that leads to repentance (2 Corinthians 7:10). Make Yourself known in real and powerful ways, Jesus, and bless _____ with a greater understanding of Who You are. If _____ has allowed his/her heart to be hardened against the knowledge of Your plan for redemption, or if he/she has opened the door to believing Satan's lies, break the powers of darkness and loose the binding chains of despair, fear, false gods or selfish ambition. Grant spiritual insight, wisdom and understanding that he/she might yearn to comprehend the supernatural realm. And grant me the opportunity and the courage to introduce _____ to You, Jesus. I pray this in Your holy name. Amen.

REFLECTIONS ON CHAPTER TWO

1. Recount a time from your life when you shared Christ's goodness with a friend. How did God orchestrate the opportunity? Take time now to pray for that person.

_____

_____

_____

_____

2. Now think about a current relationship with someone you hope to witness God's love and grace to. Write their name(s) down and begin praying for an open door and guidance to share with that person.

_____

_____

_____

_____

3. Consider the following statement from this chapter: *"Reflection on Christ's love for me helps me identify with His heart of compassion for the*

person I'm reaching out to." How does this thought inform your own love for others?

_____

_____

_____

_____

In Chapter Three, you will read more about how God uses our daily encounters with others to impart the sweet aroma of Christ's presence. It is God's work of revelation we trust as we simply listen for and respond to His guiding voice. Though the awareness we are the fragrance of Christ to others can bring a sense of awe, we rely on God's sovereignty to bring about the transformation in the lives of our friends and loved ones.

CHAPTER THREE

THE FRAGRANCE OF THE PRESENCE OF CHRIST

"For we are the aroma of Christ to God among those who
are being saved and among those who are perishing."

2 Corinthians 2:15

I sat on the edge of Alfred's bed, holding his hand and quietly praying. Despite the oxygen mask covering his mouth, he tried to interact. "You don't need to talk," I told him, "I'm just here to pray with you." This was difficult for him, because all our previous visits centered on stories from his war years. Those years were implanted in his memory, and he loved to speak about his time in World War II, when he trained military dogs. One particular German Shepherd named Duke had especially captured his heart, giving him many stories to share. Alfred was in and out of sleep this day, so I only stayed long enough to pray over him. With the little strength he had, he grasped my hand as he received my prayers.

I volunteered with a nursing home visitation ministry, and Alfred was one of my favorite residents to spend time with. A few friends and I visited once a week, walking through the hallways to talk and pray with residents. Alfred was one who preferred to stay in his room, so I usually stopped there last. A stroke had caused some stuttering problems, so listening to his stories took time. We always ended our conversations in prayer, and though he was a devout Baptist, he admitted to having a few doubts. The emotions brought on by the stroke made him especially vulnerable and honest. Responding to his doubts, I used words of truth and assurance, often quoting from Scripture. For whatever reason, Alfred held doubt about his salvation and the assurance of eternal security was still veiled, at least in part. Perhaps it was the stroke, perhaps something else, but my words of truth brought him peace.

After months of visiting Alfred, a second stroke left him in a very frail state, and I felt helpless to minister effectively. Troubled by this, I sought the advice of a church elder, Gregoria Romero. Explaining my frustrations, I wondered if I was doing any good at all. Perhaps the most well-respected woman in our church, Gregoria responded to my worries directly. "You must not give up now," she exhorted. "The presence of Christ is in you, which means when you are with Alfred, Christ is also there. Just leave God's work to the Holy Spirit, and trust the fragrance of Christ's presence will minister to his needs."

That was all I needed to hear, and I continued to visit and pray with Alfred for the next few weeks, until he passed. I believe the moments spent with him, the prayers prayed over him, the assurance of Scripture spoken to him, all unveiled more of Christ's goodness and glory, preparing him for eternity.

Whether we are involved in a nursing home ministry or encouraging a co-worker who has an inordinate amount of stress in life, we are the presence of Christ in that particular moment. Our prayers, our words, and our acts of kindness are a sweet-smelling aroma to God, as fragrant as the costly perfume with which Mary anointed Christ's feet (John 12:3). Christ's presence in us brings revelation of His goodness and tears away at the darkness and deception that clouds spiritual clarity.

But make no mistake—it is not *our* presence that removes the veil, rather Christ's presence *in us* doing the work. We are simply the conduit. And it is through the conduit of our words and prayers that others come to understand the sweet-smelling aroma of the sacrifice Christ made for them (Ephesians 5:2).

This takes away the pressure, doesn't it? Like me, do you worry yourself silly about what words to say and how they will be received? Do you imagine how specific scenarios might play out, as you fuss over exactly how to share? There is no reason for this angst because when we realize it is the Holy Spirit doing the work, we feel much less responsibility for our own inferiority of speech or wisdom (1 Corinthians 2:1). Though prone to act in our natural, human strength, we seek the peace of God's presence as we pray for the work of the Holy Spirit to act in and through us.

While I believe the fragrance of Christ flowed through me to bless Alfred, I am also confident the fragrance of Christ in Gregoria brought great insight to my soul when she counseled me. In fact, her words eventually led me to write this book. I have never forgotten the assurance she gave me, and the courage to move forward in faith. Though the veil had long been removed from my spiritual vision, I needed a deeper insight that her words facilitated.

SEEING THROUGH THE MIRROR

In Paul's letter to the Corinthians, he explains that in our human experience we only have partial vision, as if looking through a mirror.

> "For now we see in a mirror, dimly, but then face to face. Now
> I know in part; but then I shall know fully, even as I have been
> fully known."
>
> 1 Corinthians 13:12

This reminds us that even though the veil which shields our spiritual understanding has been torn in two, we still only have a partial vision, as if seeing through a glass. Our faith in the power and work of the Holy Spirit takes it from there as we spend time in God's presence.

In the verse this book is based on, *"And we all, with unveiled face, beholding the glory of the Lord, are being transformed into the same image from one degree of glory to another. For this comes from the Lord who is the Spirit"* (2 Corinthians 3:18), Paul explains that we, too, are being transformed. Unveiling spiritual wisdom and insight is a continual process of spiritual growth, which produces fruit in our lives. We simply trust God to accomplish the illumination of His goodness working in and through us to reach a sinful and fallen world. Like a peaceful flower garden intricately patterned, we are the fragrance of His goodness, exuding the Master Gardener's beautiful design.

A SIMPLE PLANTING OF SEEDS

We will never fully know or understand how God orchestrates the transformation of souls as His Spirit draws them to Him. Sometimes, the "harvest" takes years of faithful sowers planting seeds of hope and truth. Sometimes we are blessed to see the transformation, but other times we simply sow the seeds and God takes it from there, leaving us prayerfully wondering what may have happened with the person's spiritual development. God knows all the stories from start to finish, but it's a great joy when we witness how the fragrance of Christ in us breathes life and light into the darkness of souls.

A friend of mine, Pastor Jan Eitel (also founder of Hearts for the World International Ministries), often recounts the story of how his friendship with my brother, Mark, helped him turn his life around as a young adult. Mark and Jan were high school friends, sharing a love for music and drama. As dedicated musicians and performers, they hold much in common. However, in high school, Mark was a Christian, and Jan was not. In their friendship, Mark's faithful witness consistently breathed the fragrance of Christ's goodness into Jan's life.

At one point, Jan became attracted to a young woman, who was a Christian. He and the girl engaged in a conversation about love where Jan worked hard to impress her with his intellectual philosophies. She was not impressed, though, and gave Jan a Bible, asking him to go home and read the "love chapter," 1 Corinthians 13. Jan did so, and the words he read began to tear away the veil clouding spiritual understanding. His heart and spirit were troubled, and he wanted to know more.

In his confusion, Jan reached out to Mark, who advised, "Get the Bible she gave you, and read the entire gospel of John. Then go back and read it again, and then read it once more after that." Mark told Jan that in reading the gospel of John, he would come to know who Jesus was and why He came. In learning about Jesus, Mark said, Jan would understand love more deeply. And Jan did just that. In doing so, Jan began to see beyond the veil into the glorious realm of God's kingdom. Full of awe and a spiritual curiosity that could not be ignored, Jan asked Jesus to be Lord and Savior of his life.

That was over forty years ago, and since then, Jan has ministered the goodness of Christ to many people throughout the world. He and his wife, Sydney, founded Hearts for the World International Ministries, an organization that supports growing church communities in countries throughout Africa. It brings my brother great joy knowing the fragrance of Christ in him brought (and continues to bring) transformation and hope to so many. Jan's upbringing had not presented an opportunity for him to learn about Jesus; but God used Mark, and the girl Jan was trying to impress, to breathe the fragrant aroma of Christ's goodness. The beauty from this transformation continues to bring fresh awareness of God's kingdom throughout the world.

A FIELD RIPE FOR HARVEST

While it may surprise some, an increasing number of people in society today have never heard about Jesus's love for them. Perhaps they've never been told about God's redemptive plan because their primary exposure to information comes from secular and social media, rarely inclined to present God's truths. According to Pew Research Center, the percent of American adults who describe themselves as Christian has decreased by twelve percent over the period of one decade (from seventy-seven percent to sixty-five percent). Since 2008, the percentage of religiously unaffiliated has increased by seventeen percent. As of 2019, self-described atheists account for four percent of U.S. adults, with agnostics making up five percent. Additionally, seventeen percent of Americans describe their religion as "nothing in particular."[1]

In current society, some families have never entered the doors of a church and others belong to a non-Christian religion or culture where the idea of a personal God is a foreign concept. There is an enormous field, ripe for harvest right in front of us. Just as physical heart ailments create concern, so should the spiritual condition of unbelief. Christians need to seek Christ's heart of compassion more than ever. We are that wafting and inviting fragrance that catches the attention of those who walk in darkness, drawing them to a place where their hunger and thirst can be satisfied.

As we interact with others, we know prayer precedes all else, so I've included a prayer you can pray during daily encounters. The prayer is based on 1 Corinthians 2:5-14 and John 1:5.

PRAYER

Lord God, I am praying for _____. I ask that the fragrance of Your presence surround him/her on all sides, reaching to the depths of the soul. May Your Holy Spirit, who searches all things, impart words of truth into the mind of _____. Grant spiritual wisdom and understanding beyond what is possible in

1 Smith, Gregory A., Alan Cooperman, Besheer Mohamed, Elizabeth Podrebarac Sciupac, Becka A. Alper, Kiana Cox, and Claire Gecewicz. "In U.S., Decline of Christianity Continues at Rapid Pace." Pew Research Center, (October 17, 2019), accessed January 23, 2021, https://www.pewforum.org/2019/10/17/in-u-s-decline-of-christianity-continues-at-rapid-pace.

THE FRAGRANCE OF THE PRESENCE OF CHRIST   43

the natural realm so _____ might have insight into
the hidden things of the spiritual realm of Your kingdom. May
shadows disappear, and may new insights and revelations be
made clear. May truth dispel lies and may light dispel darkness.
Strengthen his/her faith and give _____ the mind
of Christ. Remove the veil hindering spiritual sight, and bring
revelation of hope, peace, direction, and comfort. Bless Your
perfect work in his/her heart, mind, body, and soul. Grant that
my interactions with _____ be a fragrant offering
before Your throne. I pray in Your precious name. Amen.

REFLECTIONS ON CHAPTER THREE

1. Recount a time in your life when you knew Christ was working in and through another person to bless you. As you think about the memory, explain what words or actions confirmed Christ's fragrance of beauty to your heart:

_____

_____

_____

_____

2. Is it difficult to embrace the knowledge that Christ's presence works and flows out of you in daily interactions with others? In what ways do you find it difficult to trust He has ordained opportunities for you to be a witness?

_____

_____

_____

_____

3. Consider the growing number of Americans who don't profess to be Christian (per the statistics referenced in this chapter). How does this reality impact your awareness of the "field ripe for harvest" in your immediate sphere of influence?

_____

_____

_____

4. Read the following Bible verses and explain how the fragrance of Christ's beauty is addressed—Ephesians 5:1-2, 2 Corinthians 2:15, Proverbs 27:9:

_____

_____

_____

As we step out in faith through the open doors God provides to share His love with others, we carry a most powerful weapon, the Word of God. Chapter Four will encourage you to wield that sword of the Spirit in confident assurance. Doing so will pierce hearts and penetrate veils.

THE POWER OF THE WORD

"For the word of God is living and active, sharper than any two-edged sword, piercing to the division of soul and of spirit, of joints and of marrow, and discerning the thoughts and intentions of the heart."

Hebrews 4:12

Whether an arrow sent to wound, or a balm intended to heal, words have power. God has ordained the use of spoken and written words to bless and to curse. Why do we call a friend when we are troubled? We seek their support and guidance through their *words*! Why do we hold onto all our favorite books? We hope to re-read the *words* that imparted an inspirational message to us on our first read. Why might we keep that scrap of paper upon which we wrote a quotation or Bible verse? We know the hopeful *words* will encourage and inspire us again and again. Words have power!

When our interactions with others include sharing scriptural truths, we are shining a light on their path (Psalm 119:105). Speaking words of truth brings God's life to hardened or hurting hearts. In the spiritual realm, where we only see through a glass, scriptural promises penetrate the veil and release wisdom and understanding. Therefore, our interactions with those who don't know Jesus should include sharing biblical assurances. We trust the power of God's Word will pierce the darkness and bring revelation and transformation.

WORDS THAT GUIDE

In my career as an educator I've worked in various roles at several schools. A few years ago, I started at a new school, and as a morning person I was usually first in the building. Regularly, I began my workday praying through the hallways, sometimes stepping inside a classroom or an office space to pray more intentionally. After several weeks of doing this, I found God daily prompting me to stop and pray specifically for one teacher, Glenda (not her actual name). I'd heard gossip about her personal struggles and how they affected her work performance. As I prayed over her desk, God gave me Scriptures to leave, so I began carrying a little notepad of sticky notes with me. As God gave me a verse to share, I'd post a note with the Scripture on her computer. I also prayed for an opportunity to share more personally.

Things went from bad to worse for Glenda as the struggles in her personal life caused greater problems. One afternoon at a weekly staff meeting she sat down next to me and I sensed an open door. The meeting addressed one of many troublesome issues facing schools. Jokingly, I commented to those sitting at my table, "*This* is why I pray through the hallways of our school every day." Glenda smiled and told me she thought it was nice I took the time to do so. I mentioned I was the one leaving her Scripture verses each day. She brightened and said they meant a lot to her.

Soon, it was clear she was in jeopardy of losing her job, so I asked Glenda if she would like to get together to pray. We met after school. I could tell she was hesitant, nervous and broken. She explained her faith to me, saying she was a spiritual person who believed the "universe" was always watching over her. I responded with God's prompted words, "It seems to me this is a pretty vague concept of God. It might be difficult to know what is really true by seeking answers from such an undefined entity as the universe." She paused and considered my words thoughtfully. I continued, "What if God were more defined? In fact, what if God wanted a personal relationship with you?" Glenda reacted with a receptive and intrigued smile, and I knew God was knocking on the door of her heart.

We prayed together that day, and during other opportunities that followed. Her struggles continued, but she came to an understanding that God was bigger and more personal than the universe. Like so many people, Glenda had bought into a common and popular misconception of God. Satan's lie that the comfortable, ambiguous belief in the "universe" is sufficient veiled her spiritual understanding and needed to be confronted through prayer and the truth of God's Word.

WORDS THAT COMFORT

My friend, Crystal (not her actual name), experiences the horrible effects of childhood trauma and abuse from the hands of a trusted adult. She is a precious and loving person who suffers with nightmares and other forms of Post-Traumatic Stress Disorder (PTSD). Years ago, after we first met, we got together for lunch regularly to pray and talk. Eventually, with some guidance, she prayed the prayer of salvation. The deep wounds in her soul cause Crystal to grapple with comprehending Jesus's love and grace. Like many victims of abuse, she guards her feelings and focuses on establishing safe routines and structures to get through the day.

While it took time, Crystal learned to trust our friendship. Nowadays we live in different cities, but she still reaches out during seasons when the struggle is especially hard. When those times come, I seek God's help to know how to speak hope, truth and assurance to her. And God is powerfully faithful to give me Scriptures to pray and words to say to assure her of His great love and promises for healing.

I often wonder what I would do if I didn't have a plethora of Scriptures at my fingertips for the times I need to speak into her life. I am in awe of the many Bible verses I can pray over and share with her as the Holy Spirit leads. And though I may not know how deeply Crystal comprehends the power of these words, I am certain those spoken assurances reach the depths of her soul, even if her emotional state prevents a thorough understanding.

It is easier to speak words of truth into another person's life when they already know Christ. For Christians, imparting Scripture to each other binds us together like a three-strand cord (Ecclesiastes 4:12). However, sharing with a person who doesn't know Christ can be awkward since we are unsure how they will react. But when we share intentionally as opportunities arise, we seldom regret it. Praying and watching for those open doors is an integral part of living out the ministry of the unveiled face. Because Satan continually works to deceive others and cause unbelief, speaking God's words of truth into their lives is a weapon to counteract his evil schemes and strategies.

THE SWORD OF THE SPIRIT

The Bible tells us Satan prowls around like a roaring lion seeking someone to devour (1 Peter 5:8), and in the Gospel of John, Jesus describes Satan as a thief who comes only to steal, kill and destroy (John 10:10). The evil one is active in this world, doing everything possible to blind spiritual vision. He is the author of lies (John 8:44), and those lies create a veil that shields understanding. There is a battle raging, and we need a powerful weapon in our hands to fight effectively. The Bible tells us the Word of God is sharper than any two-edged sword, able to divide spirit from soul (Hebrews 4:12). When the truth of Scripture is spoken to (or over) a misguided or hurting soul, we have the confident assurance of its power to confront deception and to heal wounds.

STRONGHOLDS IN OUR THINKING

Even for Christians, the battle in our minds is challenging. Few would argue controlling thoughts can be difficult, and we often fall prey to believing the lies the enemy plants in our minds. These lies can become a stronghold of unbelief seemingly impossible to overcome. Confronting lies with words of truth is critical to bring deliverance from such strongholds. Scriptures counteract every falsehood, and unless truth is spoken in the face of the enemy's deceptions, the roots of unbelief grow deeper. (See "A Note About Unbelief," Appendix A, page 101).

If this battle is hard for Christians, imagine how impossible it is for non-believers. The thought patterns circulating in their minds take them down a treacherous path to emptiness and hopelessness. But God has equipped us with a powerful weapon, and even simple responses in personal conversations referencing an applicable Scripture will dispel lies in the unseen realms. It is spiritual warfare as we wield the sword of the Spirit to bring down strongholds of evil (2 Corinthians 10:5).

With such a wealth of truth at our fingertips, using our knowledge of Scripture in God-ordained interactions is an effective and vital part of the ministry of the unveiled face. We can be unafraid to tell others what the Bible says, trusting words of truth will release those imprisoned to sin, shame and unbelief.

WORDS RECEIVED IN FAITH

The writer of Hebrews reminds us to pray that spoken words of truth are received in faith.

> "For good news came to us just as to them, but the message they heard did not benefit them, because ***they were not united by faith with those who listened***."

> Hebrews 4:2 (emphasis added)

The word "united" translates more directly to "commingled," helping us see how critical it is to receive God's words in faith. So when we pray for others, we intentionally ask for a uniting (or commingling) with faith. Often I will pray for a blessing of faith to be instilled in the heart and mind of the person I'm ministering to. The Holy Spirit, the giver of all gifts, will be faithful to provide this increased measure of faith. Along those lines, what follows is a prayer you can pray for those God calls you to minister to. Specific Scriptures are referenced in the prayer as a model.

PRAYER

Thank You, Almighty God that Your Word is truth and brings life and power into the souls of others as we speak and pray over them. I pray now for _____ and ask for the truth of Your Word to remove the veil of unbelief that clouds his/her spiritual vision. I ask for open doors and opportunities for the truth to open blind eyes and bring freedom to the captive (Isaiah 61:1). Bless _____ with the gift of faith, that the words of truth might be received with assurance, and that a spirit of unbelief would be bound on Earth as it is in Heaven (Matthew 18:18). Your Word is living and active and sharper than any two-edged sword, piercing as far as the division of soul and spirit, of both joints and marrow, and able to judge the thoughts and intentions of the heart (Hebrews 4:12). I ask that the lies of the enemy would be bound and erased from _____'s mind and that the power of Your Word take deep root into the soil of his/her soul. Your Word is upright and all Your works are done in faithfulness (Psalm 33:4).You spoke the world into being and it was so, Lord (Psalm 33:9). Now speak life and redemption into _____, that he/she might know Your goodness and understand Your plan. May the eyes of his/her heart be enlightened to know the hope of Your calling, the riches of Your glorious inheritance and Your incomparably great power for those who believe (Ephesians 1:18). In Your name I pray. Amen.

REFLECTIONS ON CHAPTER FOUR

1. Take some time to dissect the verse in this chapter's heading (Hebrews 4:12). What do you think Paul means when he says, "The word of God can pierce through to the division of soul and spirit"? _____

_____

_____

_____

_____

2. Re-read Ephesians 6, where the Apostle Paul describes the armor of God, including the sword of the spirit. Visualize an experience you've had, or hope to have, witnessing to a friend or loved one. Describe how you envision each piece of the armor coming into play in this interaction: _____

_____

_____

_____

_____

_____

3. Consider how unbelief can prevent people from seeking to see Jesus, beyond the veil that blinds them to the spiritual realm. What verses and considerations from this chapter might guide you in your relationships with those who choose to embrace doubt and unbelief? _____

_____

_____

_____

4. Take time now to list some Bible verses that come to mind about the dangers of unbelief, including those shared in this chapter. Commit to memorizing a few of those verses:

_____

_____

_____

By this point in the book, I hope you have a basic understanding of the ministry of the unveiled face. The next chapter, "Our Sphere of Influence," addresses the various places and situations we find ourselves in where opportunities exist to walk out this ministry.

CHAPTER FIVE

OUR SPHERE OF INFLUENCE

"Walk in wisdom toward outsiders, making the best use of the time.
Let your speech always be gracious, seasoned with salt,
so that you may know how you ought to answer each person."

Colossians 4:5-6

Going to the grocery store always makes me a bit grumpy since I'm old enough to remember the days when customer service was a greater priority than it is now. I'm troubled by the negative and critical thoughts running through my mind when I have to bag my own groceries or use the self-check-out line. I grumble as I navigate increasingly narrow aisles full of stockers blocking my way. Despite my complaining, God uses the struggle to remind me even a grocery store provides opportunity to be salt and light to the world. I endeavor to view my shopping experiences through this lens as I pray for and speak kindly to those I would rather scowl at.

I write this chapter during the year 2020, a year no one will forget. The COVID-19 pandemic changed the familiarity of routine dramatically. Among other adjustments, we've been forced to modify our way of interacting with others. Having to "social distance" ourselves from others has brought online and virtual interactions to the forefront. We grieve the lack of in-person contact, and worry the masks we wear in public inhibit our sharing of love, even with a simple smile. Yet, this is reality, and if we look at our current circumstances through God's eyes, we still see plenty of open doors and opportunities for the ministry of the unveiled face, like the grocery store!

THE INFLUENCE OF SOCIAL MEDIA

Social media is one example providing the opportunity for conversations that may not surface elsewhere. Through social media, I've reconnected with people from my past I would have lost touch with otherwise. It is far from ideal, but worldwide access to various forms of digital communication has become integral to human communication.

Recently, an old high school friend (a very thoughtful, humanistic thinker) posed a question on her Facebook page to all who would engage. Christine (not her actual name) asked if anyone still believed in hell. The conversation stream had many commenters, but I was one of a very few who held an actual belief in hell. As impersonal as the written exchanges felt, it was an open door. I prayed and entered in.

Below are a few excerpts from that Facebook stream (note: it does not include all the responses, only the interchanges between Christine and me).

CHRISTINE: Do you believe in Hell? Why or why not?

ME: Sadly, yes; but more importantly, I believe in God's amazing plan of redemption making it possible to have victory over sin, death, and hell through the free offer of salvation by accepting Jesus Christ's loving sacrifice to take our place. Wondering why you picked this topic?

CHRISTINE: I picked the topic because I don't believe in hell as it was presented to us as children in church, yet I believe there is something to the concept, and I'd love to hear others' thoughts.

ME: A different way of processing your topic is to assume hell IS real; and then process the wondering, "If hell is real, how would

I (or others) live differently? Hell, being defined as eternal separation from a loving and sovereign God.

CHRISTINE: Do you really think fear of punishment is the right motivation for being a kind person? I'm just not a big believer in coercion. It may change behavior, but it won't change hearts.

ME: I'm not sure what you are saying is coercive? But I think you are saying the belief in hell acts as a deterrent to sinful living because it would mean one would spend eternity being punished? (Hope I'm interpreting your comment correctly). I find this conversation stream both heartbreaking and intriguing. Determining whether or not there is a hell based on human opinion and human understanding is a bit shortsighted, but I understand we live in an age of truth being relative to whatever individuals define truth to be ("relative" truth is an oxymoron, isn't it?)

For me, hell is eternal separation from a loving God (so, yes, that would mean the ultimate horror/punishment). God gives every chance for every soul on Earth to accept His grace and forgiveness by accepting Jesus as Lord, and acknowledging God's sovereignty. That seems to be the more important issue. Hell is not the issue really (though I know you presented it as such). For me, grace and God's sovereignty is the issue and it will forever boggle my mind why so many choose not to receive grace, mercy, joy, peace, etc. from a sovereign Lord. Hope that makes sense to you. Written word is tricky to understand fully another person's meaning.

CHRISTINE: What I meant by coercion is essentially "Be good or else." If that makes sense. (In this case, fear of hell being the "or else.")

ME: So, that presumes God's strategy is coercive and based on humanity's ability to "be good" as you say. Consider the opposite, if you will. What if, God's plan simply acknowledged evil exists in a fallen world, so there needed to be a way for people to still have relationship with the holy Creator? Instead of our having to "be good or else," we are invited into communing with God through Jesus Christ. I know quoting Scripture will not mean much to you, but there are so many verses in the Bible to support this supposition. Here's just one: "For all have sinned and fall short of the glory of God, and are justified by His grace as a gift through the redemption that is in Christ Jesus." (Romans 3:23-24)

There was no further reply from Christine.

Perhaps I went too far in this conversation, but I present the exchange as an example of opportunities social media provides to speak truth and share God's Word with others. Social media is far from the best method of communication, but it is one of many open doors God can utilize. In my social media presence, I intentionally share Scriptures and expressions of truth and encouragement. With every post, I pray it reaches the hearts of those God intends. It is one simple method of speaking truth and light into a fallen and confused world.

An integral part of the ministry of the unveiled face is being ready and responsive to all encounters, whether through social media interactions, at the grocery store, or by helping a neighbor with yardwork. Our sphere of influence is in God's hands, and it is fluid because God moves us through varying places in the seasons of life. The workplace, our schools and neighborhoods, and a multitude of service opportunities all have different lengths of involvement. Consider each moment or season as "assignments" if you will, or even "divine appointments" with limited periods of time. With each opportunity, we have a chance to minister compassion and truth.

THE GREAT COMMISSION AND THE GREAT COMPASSION

A minister friend of mine, Rev. Dale Rosenberger, talks about the inseparability between Christ's Great Commission and Christ's Great

Compassion. The familiar verse in Matthew 28 issues the Great Commission to proclaim the Gospel message.

> "Go therefore and make disciples of all nations, baptizing them in the name of the Father and of the Son and of the Holy Spirit, teaching them to observe all that I have commanded you. And behold, I am with you always, to the end of the age."

> Matthew 28:19-20

What Dale calls the *Great Compassion* can be further understood by the Gospel passages where Jesus calls His disciples to more concrete and practical service (Matthew 25:35-40). Tangible acts of care and concern go hand in hand with our prayerful and verbal witness. Dale's imperative reminds us we must hold both calls to ministry with intention, so our words of witness are united with acts of service done in Christ's name. When we feed the hungry and take care of the sick, the orphan and the widow, we are participating in the spiritual realm. Compassionate acts of service for others open doors that help build relationship. As trust is built, people are more receptive to hear about and receive Christ. Our words, prayers and acts of service bring an unveiling for those who may not yet know Christ.[2]

I have participated in a handful of short-term mission trips through Habitat for Humanity, International (locations were in Mexico, Nicaragua, and Guatemala). These were transforming experiences with a lifelong impact. But for the communities served by our "team," our influence only lasted ten to twelve days. During each trip, we worked, ate, sang, worshipped, and prayed with the families whose homes we helped construct. In some situations, we partied with them. We assisted watching over and supporting the children of each community, and we received blessings they offered us as we hoped they were blessed in return. Many nights during those trips, I laid awake praying

---

2   Dale Rosenberger, discussion with the author, November 18, 2020

through the night (sleeping arrangements were never very comfortable). Praying on the soil of another nation offers an opportunity for tremendous impact and I felt God's prompting to pray in powerful ways.

When the day of departure came, tears poured as we bid farewell and left our new friends in God's mighty hands. Through our limited time of service, we instilled hope in lives where God was mightily at work. Our service as well as our words and prayers provided a revelation of God's goodness and glory.

MUDDLING THROUGH SPHERES OF INFLUENCE

Do we always get it right? Of course not. We are fallible humans navigating our way through an unseen, spiritual realm. We come before God as poor in spirit seeking to understand the ways of His kingdom. Our understanding is limited, for now we see through a glass (1 Corinthians 13:12). Therefore, we place our imperfections at His feet and ask for grace and strength to move forward as He leads.

Sometimes we don't hear Him precisely. Sometimes we move forward in our own strength, confused about His timing. Sometimes, we dig in our heels obstinately and give Him a flat out, "No, God. I'm too tired, or I'm too afraid." Regardless of our hesitancies, we always come back to the place where mercy wraps us up in the blanket of God's sovereignty. There is no condemnation. In childlike faith, we continue to seek His voice with greater clarity, knowing His presence transcends every situation, whether of our own making or His divine appointment. The more we come before God in humility and repentance, the sweeter His voice becomes. His steadfast and continual transformative work in our own hearts will deepen our devotion and strengthen our trust. God's ways and thoughts are far bigger than we can fathom in our humanity. But, greater trust in His faithfulness always leads to obedience.

In the autumn years of my teaching career, I experienced what one might call a professional crisis. Thinking I was fulfilling a bucket list endeavor, I accepted a position as a middle school language arts teacher (previously, I had only taught elementary). It turned out to be a poor choice as I soon realized I had thrown myself to the wolves, and they were eating me alive. The behavior management and relationship building strategies that worked in elementary school came up lacking with these streetwise thirteen- and fourteen-year-olds.

While I'd like to forget nearly every moment of that school year, I choose to remember moments like the mornings I supervised the mayhem in the hallways as students ran, yelled, pushed, and cursed at each other while at their lockers. Calmly, I'd stand—like the other teachers in my hallway—to ensure they knew adults were watching. But, perhaps unlike the other teachers, I also prayed. I'd pray for each student by name, asking God to help them find their true identity in Him.

I also used dialogue journals (a strategy for modeling writing skills). In these daily back-and-forth diaries, I'd learn a bit more about students' hopes, fears, and families. Knowing I would not last long in the position, I threw caution to the wind and often wrote about God as I felt led.

I tell this difficult story to impart the message that I survived by God's grace. While I may have jumped ahead of God in taking the position, I sometimes wonder if He had me just where He wanted for that season. It was a time full of tears, panic attacks, and feelings of absolute failure. I look back on it now, knowing I was being shaped in a fiery furnace. It was a season through which I learned to listen more closely to God's voice. He never abandoned me; and as only He can do, He still worked in and through me, as I sought to serve Him.

THE PRIESTHOOD OF ALL BELIEVERS

As Christians, we are conduits of God's kingdom wherever we are and regardless of the people we're with. The priesthood of all believers is a doctrine (accredited to Martin Luther) supporting the ministry of the unveiled face. In our fallible and frail humanity, we serve a powerful and transcendent Lord, collectively and individually. As you will read in the next chapter, each one of us is a priest of the Most High God because of the New Covenant gift of the cross.

Rachel Ciano, writing for *Credo Magazine*, explains the concept of the priesthood of all believers. *"All who have faith in Christ and are baptized are designated priests and share in Christ's royal priesthood . . . every believer has equal access to the Father through Jesus. The corollary is that every believer has the responsibility to act as a priest to other believers, to minister to them, particularly through proclaiming Scripture to them."*[3]

Embracing our assignment as priest, we walk in the confident assurance God will use us to bless and speak truth to others in all spheres of influence. With every opportunity, we know God is sovereign to work in us, through us, and in spite of us, certain to transform us along the way. Each day is a new opportunity to minister as God leads.

The sample prayer that follows can be prayed as a personal plea or a prayer for all believers. It is my constant heart cry.

PRAYER

Jesus, grant open doors and opportunities to be light and salt in this fallen world. Open my eyes and heart to enter in to the time, place, and need that You have ordained. I trust Your timing for these divine appointments. Bless me with words to speak and prayers to pray that will bring the awakening needed. Help me see and respond to every opportunity for however long You have me in a situation. Grant me perseverance in prayer and service. As I do my best to be Your priest, release the enlightenment and revelation that will remove the veil that shields understanding of Your goodness and glory. In Your name, I pray. Amen.

---

3   Ciano, Rachel, "Luther's Doctrine of the Priesthood of All Believers: The Importance for Today," *Credo Magazine*, accessed Jan. 8, 2020, https://credomag.com/2020/01/luthers-doctrine-of-the-priesthood-of-all-believers-the-importance-for-today.

REFLECTIONS ON CHAPTER FIVE

1. Consider these thoughts from the chapter regarding the priesthood of all believers: *Embracing our assignment as priest, we walk in the confident assurance God will use us to bless and speak truth to others in all spheres of influence. With every opportunity, we know God is sovereign to work in us, through us, and in spite of us, certain to transform us along the way.* How do these statements inform you about your role as priest?

_____

_____

_____

_____

2. Recount a time (or times) in your life when you knew God worked in and through you to impact the lives of others. How did both the Great Commission and the Great Compassion come into play during that season?

_____

_____

_____

_____

3. As you consider some of the specific areas where you can be the unveiled face to others, jot down names of people God places on your heart in these places. Be sure to pray the prayer above for each one:

Social Media: _____

Workplace: _____

Neighborhood: _____

Family: _____

Friends: _____

Community and Service Opportunities: _____

Other (list them here): _____

_____

_____

_____

_____

_____

_____

CHAPTER SIX

BEHIND THE VEIL: THE RADIANCE OF CHRIST

"He is the radiance of the glory of God and the exact imprint of his nature, and he upholds the universe by the word of his power."

Hebrews 1:3

How does one describe the realm where you come face to face with the presence of the living Lord? The radiance that lies behind the veil is difficult to explain with mere words. Scripture tells us Christ is the true light which enlightens every man (John 1:9), and He dwells in unapproachable light (1 Timothy 6:16). Envision a realm with brilliant, emanating light from which radiates an inexpressible perfection. As the veil is removed, a penetrating and eternal presence envelops the soul with the deepest grace and compassion. This indescribable realm is a safe haven; a refuge where strength and hope are discovered.

While it is true that we only see through a glass here on earth (1 Corinthians 13:12), we can trust God to continually reveal new mysteries from behind the veil as we grow in our faith. Christ imparts spiritual fruits and gifts moment by moment to all who are eager to receive. Uncovering the multitude of promises and assurances is like opening an enormous and bottomless treasure chest. It is an amazing journey. We discover the mysteries of God's kingdom, and those mysteries enlighten us to understand God's glory in a deeper way than we ever thought possible.

OLD COVENANT: GOD'S SHEKINAH GLORY

To better understand this radiance, it may be helpful to recall manifestations of God's Shekinah glory in both the Old and New Testaments. *Shekinah* is a Hebrew word meaning "dwelling," and Shekinah glory is a visible manifestation of the divine presence of God on Earth. Under the Old Covenant, a sacred and holy inner sanctuary housed the Ark of the Covenant where the glory and presence of the Lord dwelt. The Ark of the Covenant was protected in a tabernacle inside a tent (Exodus 25:22) and only the high priests could enter. Only the high priest could behold God's manifest presence.

During the time of Moses when the ordinances of the Old Covenant—the Ten Commandments—were first imparted, the manifest presence of God appeared in a supernatural, but visible, cloud hovering over Mt. Sinai. At this moment, the prophet Moses ascended the mountains and entered into this ominous cloud to meet with the Most High God.

Imagine standing alone on Mt. Sinai when the sky darkened and God's Shekinah glory descended like a cloud. There Moses interceded for the Israelites, beseeching God to send His presence with them on the journey to the Promised Land . . . beseeching God to reveal His glory. Moses needed the assurance of God's glory to embark on the epic journey.

What gave Moses the courage to ask God to reveal His *glory*? Having already witnessed God's manifest presence in a burning bush, Moses knew God more intimately than any human could. With courage that can only come from desperation, Moses pleaded with God to reveal His glory. In response to this bold request, God answered Moses, saying, "I will make all My *goodness* pass before you" (Exodus 33:18 emphasis added).

Because no one could look upon the face of God and survive, God told Moses to hide in the cleft of the rock on Mt. Sinai as His goodness passed.

How fascinating it is when Moses asked to see God's *glory*, God responded by revealing His *goodness*. Could it be that the primary attribute of God's glory is His goodness? How awe-inspiring it is to realize the brilliant and penetrating light behind the veil *is* the very radiance of God's *goodness*.

Charles Spurgeon addresses Moses' experience in his famous sermon, A View of God's Glory:

> I can picture Moses as he stood in that cleft of the rock with the hand of God before his eyes, and I can see him look as man never looked before, confident in faith, yet more than confounded at himself that he could have asked such a petition. Now, what attribute is God about to show to Moses? His petition is, "Show me thy glory." Will he show him his justice? Will he show him his holiness? Will he show his wrath? Will he show him his power? Will he break yon cedar and show him he is almighty? Will he rend yonder mountain and show him that he can be angry? Will he bring his sins to remembrance, and show that he is omniscient? No; hear the still small voice—"I will make all my goodness pass before thee." Ah! The goodness of God is God's glory. God's greatest glory is that he is good. The brightest gem in the crown of God is his goodness.[4]

After beholding God's Shekinah glory, Moses had to veil his face because the Israelites could not endure looking at the radiance still resting upon him. Imagine the sheer brightness emanating from Moses as he descended Mt. Sinai. Being confronted with such wonder surely would have caused the people to fall prostrate in repentance before a Holy God.

As we read of the Israelites' journey to the Promised Land, it is clear they were afraid of God's presence because of their sin. Unwilling to fully repent, they continued to fall into sinful habits. They preferred to let Moses commune with God on their behalf. No doubt their conscience convicted them of their disobedience, and who wants to confront the darkness of rebellion?

---

4   Spurgeon, C.H. "A View of God's Glory," a sermon by C.H. Spurgeon, accessed July 11, 2020, https://archive.spurgeon.org/sermons/3120.php.

The same dichotomy exists today. We acknowledge God, are aware of our sin, yet continually choose to rebel. We resist genuine repentance, and are afraid of experiencing an intimate encounter with Almighty God.

NEW COVENANT SHEKINAH GLORY

Under the Old Covenant, the way to atone for and be cleansed from sin was through sacrifice and ritual—something the people wanted Moses and high priests to take care of on their behalf. But as the writer of Hebrews emphasizes, we are now under the New Covenant, where we have continual and unfathomable access to God's presence through Christ Jesus, the perfect and final high priest. The book of Hebrews explains the New Covenant promise thoroughly.

> "Therefore, brethren, since we have confidence to enter the holy place by the blood of Jesus, by a new and living way which He inaugurated for us through the veil, that is, His flesh, and since we have a great priest over the house of God, let us draw near with a sincere heart in full assurance of faith, having our hearts sprinkled clean from an evil conscience and our bodies washed with pure water."

> Hebrews 10:19-22 (NASB1995)

This glorious revelation of God's goodness is freely given to those who humbly seek to know and serve him. Drawing near to God is the very essence of Christianity under the New Covenant. While the Old Covenant law was given through Moses, grace and truth (of the New Covenant) were realized through Christ (John 1:17). When the time was right for the New Covenant to unfold as Jesus walked upon the Earth, Shekinah glory was revealed strategically again.

This unveiled radiance is what John the Baptist saw descending from Heaven when the Holy Spirit in the form of a dove rested upon Jesus at baptism. In that moment, God gave John a glimpse behind the veil. As Jesus approached John to be baptized, John's human nature reasoned he was unworthy to baptize the Son of God; but when Jesus spoke about the necessity to fulfill all righteousness, the light of his goodness was revealed. And when the Holy Spirit descended, God made His glory known (Matthew 3:13-16).

Peter, John, and James witnessed this same radiance at the transfiguration upon the mountain where the brightness of God's Shekinah glory descended in a cloud and Elijah and Moses met with Jesus. These disciples did not fully comprehend the events, and the experience would only be understood after Christ's resurrection through the guidance of the Holy Spirit (Matthew 17:1-9).

The consummation of the unveiling of Christ's radiance occurred when the thick and heavy curtain to the inner sanctuary of the temple in Jerusalem ripped in two as Jesus took His final breath at crucifixion (Mark 15:38). By the sheer power of the culmination of God's redemptive plan, Jesus' death opened an immediate, unhindered path into the Father's presence. In that instant, the unfathomable realm behind the veil became immediately available to all who believed in Jesus Christ as Lord and Savior.

THE RESTING PLACE OF GOD'S GOODNESS

And now, as we carry out the Great Commission, we minister this hope and promise to others—the resting place of God's goodness is found when giving one's heart to Jesus. The moment the heart receives the Living Christ, the veil opens and the new believer can forever behold the glory of God. Jesus, the final and eternal high priest has now made us all priests who can come before the throne of Heaven to seek God's help and to intercede for others— the priesthood of all believers.

What lies behind the veil is the spiritual realm, so desperately needed by those bound in the frailties of humanity. We need not fear this place of glory. The assuring words, so often read in Bible passages, *"Do not fear,"* remind us God's presence is a gift meant to equip us in our service to Him, not to terrify us. And as we serve God, we invite others to also yield their lives to the living Lord.

This is the ministry of the unveiled face. We behold, as in a mirror, the glory of God in the spiritual realm, and we lead others to that same beholding. Like the moon reflects the sun, we reflect the radiance of Christ. We are a city on a hill giving light to the world (Matthew 5:14). In the midst of a crooked and perverse generation, we point those living in darkness to the realm where they can encounter the light of Christ (Philippians 2:15). In these earthen vessels, we help others behold and experience the grace offered for their own redemption.

Oswald Chambers describes the beauty of this daily ministry:

> "The greatest characteristic a Christian can exhibit is this completely unveiled openness before God, which allows that person's life to become a mirror for others. When the Spirit fills us, we are transformed, and by beholding God we become mirrors."[5]

Revelations of the spiritual realm come as part of our sanctification in Christ and at the decree of our sovereign Lord. While we only see through a glass right now, we can still pray the words the Holy Spirit gives us as we kneel in prayer at the throne of Heaven. Those words of promise and truth move the heavens in ways we cannot fathom. May everyone you pray for and interact with be blessed with impartations of God's glorious light.

Let the following prayer guide your intercession.

PRAYER

> God of goodness and glory, thank You for bringing redemption to humanity, and thank You that everyone has access to Your very presence. Jesus, You are our benevolent high priest

---

5   Chambers, O. *The Golden book of Oswald Chambers: My Utmost for His highest; selections for the year*, Transformed by Beholding. New York: Dodd, Mead & Company, 1935.

making a way to know and experience Your grace and mercy. As I take my place seated with you in the heavenly realm, I intercede for _____, and ask You to tear open the veil which blinds him/her to truth. Reveal Your kingdom, Jesus. Reveal the light of Your goodness. Open blind eyes to the spiritual realm. I also ask that the words of truth in my prayers for and interactions with _____ unleash angel armies to destroy the works of evil coming against him/her. Let _____ no longer be deceived, Jesus, and help him/her to receive the gospel message in faith and in the assurance that You are the perfect high priest who has made that once-and-for-all sacrifice for sin. In Your name, I pray. Amen.

REFLECTIONS ON CHAPTER SIX

1. Imagine yourself explaining the difference between the Old and New Covenant to someone. What would you say? How would you include insights about God's Shekinah glory?

_____

_____

_____

_____

_____

2. Now imagine yourself explaining the spiritual realm to that same person. How would you help them understand this realm and the gift of access we have to what lies behind the veil?

_____

_____

_____

_____

_____

3. Many Bible passages describe the revelation of God's Shekinah glory (many are given in this chapter). Choose a few that are meaningful to you and explain how they bless you:

_____

_____

_____

_____

4. Does it surprise you to consider that God's *glory* is revealed in God's *goodness*? Re-read the excerpt from Charles Spurgeon given in this chapter and explain how your awareness of God's glory has been deepened:

_____

_____

_____

_____

While Chapter Five explored our tangible spheres of influence, we now delve into the spiritual realm of influence—persevering prayer. In the natural, we can be only in one place at one time. But through prayer, God brings our service to the height, depth, and breadth of both seen and unseen realms. All people and places are seen and known by Him, but we, too, can impact all times and places through prayer. Read more on prayer in Chapter Seven.

GROUNDED IN
PERSEVERING PRAYER

"And this is the confidence that we have toward him,
that if we ask anything according to his will he hears us."

1 John 5:14

Walking out the ministry of the unveiled face is a daily call to reflect the goodness of Christ through opportune interactions with others. Being responsive in unplanned encounters is integral. This is certainly also true for defined ministries, and we are thankful for those more organized avenues to serve. Many come to know Christ through churches, mission organizations and ministries like the Billy Graham Evangelical Association, for example. According to Lifeway Research, an estimated 2.2 million people responded to invitations to become Christians throughout the fifty-eight (1947-2005) years Billy Graham preached at his crusades.[6] And more continue to respond as the crusades continue.

Billy Graham once said, "Sometimes I'm asked to list the most important steps in preparing for an evangelistic mission, and my reply is always the same: Prayer, prayer, prayer."[7] For every Billy Graham Crusade, believers intercede

---

6   "Billy Graham's Life and Ministry by the numbers," (Feb 21, 2018), Lifeway Research, accessed Feb. 8, 2021, https://lifewayresearch.com/2018/02/21/billy-grahams-life-ministry-by-the-numbers.

7   Etheridge, Kristy, "Inside a BGEA Crusade: Prayer, Preparation and More Prayer," (Jan. 7, 2014), accessed Feb. 8, 2021, https://billygraham.org/story/inside-a-bgea-crusade-prayer-preparation-and-more-prayer.

on behalf of those who attend. I often wonder if those prayer warriors understand the full extent of the call on their lives to petition Heaven for the divine encounters occurring at the crusades. Possibly only a few realize their intercession is an anointed call; still, they are faithful to pray for God's revelation and unveiling. Intercession is a strong foundation for ministry.

CONTINUAL INTERCESSION

Whether you are walking out the daily call to be a witness of Christ's grace through opportune moments, or whether you are involved in an organized ministry, persevering prayer can move mountains! Though we do not fully understand the power of prayer, we know our faithfulness in bringing petitions to God is just as powerful in our daily interactions with others as it is with more formal, organized ministry. It would be careless to assume we might reflect Christ's goodness to someone without first praying for them, and continuing to pray, and then praying even more!

I have several friends and loved ones I intercede for regularly, knowing God hears each utterance, but also understanding the importance of persisting in asking for His work to be accomplished in their lives. For whatever reason, God calls and empowers us to stand in the gap for others (Ezekiel 22:30). Not just once, but repeatedly.

Equipped by the power of the Holy Spirit, we keep presenting requests to God, continually knocking on the door of Heaven like the parable of the widow and the judge in Luke 18:1-8. Jesus told this parable to emphasize God's promise of bringing justice to those who are steadfast in prayer. The widow knew a feeble plea for assistance was not enough and she relentlessly continued to plead her case before the judge.

E.M. Bounds elevates the need for persevering prayer,

> The more praying there is in the world the better the world will be, the mightier the forces against evil everywhere. Prayer, in one phase of its operation, is a disinfectant and a preventive.

It purifies the air; it destroys the contagion of evil. Prayer is no fitful, short-lived thing. It is no voice crying unheard and unheeded in the silence. It is a voice which goes into God's ear, and it lives as long as God's ear is open to holy pleas, as long as God's heart is alive to holy things. God shapes the world by prayer. Prayers are deathless. The lips that uttered them may be closed in death, the heart that felt them may have ceased to beat, but the prayers live before God, and God's heart is set on them and prayers outlive the lives of those who uttered them; outlive a generation, outlive an age, outlive a world.[8]

MEETING WITH CHRIST IN PRAYER

It may be difficult to engage in sustained intercession, and we often feel unworthy or incapable of effective supplication. Approaching God in prayer, however, is a great privilege. The Apostle Paul tells us because we are in Christ we are seated with Him in the heavenly places, having access to the throne of Christ (Ephesians 2:6; Hebrews 1:3). These verses create an image we can visualize as we intercede for others.

When I pray, I envision the heavenly realms where Christ sits at the right hand of God. I visualize kneeling at His feet to bring my petitions before Him. Access to heaven's throne is a gift of God's unfathomable grace because of Christ's reconciliation work on our behalf. The more we visualize ourselves in the presence of Jesus, the deeper our understanding of God's kingdom. Our times of prayer are intimate moments of sweet fellowship with our Savior. Knowing God hears every heart cry assures us of His great love and His desire to commune with us.

In his book, *Intercessory Prayer*, Dutch Sheets describes intercession as meeting with God. Our "meeting" is possible because Jesus is already seated at the right hand of God interceding on our behalf. Christ's intercession allows us the access to present supplications. Building upon the Greek word

---

8   Edward M. Bounds, *The Complete Works of E.M. Bounds on Prayer* (Grand Rapids, MI: Baker Book House, 1990), 299.

for meeting (*paga*), Sheets helps us envision our part in reconciling the world to God.

> Our meeting with God is to effect another meeting—a reconciliation. We meet with Him asking Him to meet with someone else. We become the go-between . . . . Through our praying intercession, we release the fruit of what He did through His act of intercession. We bring individuals to God in prayer asking the Father to meet with them. We, too, have been given the ministry of reconciliation. Whether for a person or a nation, regardless of the reason, when we're used to create a meeting between God and humans, releasing the fruit of Christ's work, paga (Greek for "meeting") has happened.[9]

Prayer is a time of meeting with our Lord and sharing our concerns for those He brings to mind. Like unloading a burden in conversation with a friend, we know Jesus will listen and walk us through our worries. Don't we often encourage our Christian friends by telling them to "give it to Jesus," and "Let go and let God"? Though these exhortations remind us not to carry burdens in our own strength, we must not lose sight of the privilege of *sharing* the concern with Christ.

In our intercession for others, the "burden" we feel for them is carried by the only one who can save souls. But rather than viewing the "letting go" as no longer having to "deal" with the burden, we realize our prayers join with Christ's. We intercede for others like the friends of the paralytic in the Gospel of Luke (Luke 5:17-26). Frustrated by the large crowd and desperate to help their companion, they literally removed the roof of a home to lower their loved one to where Jesus could touch and heal him. Those friends were driven to do whatever it took to present the need for healing before Christ.

If we envision ourselves seated in Heaven with our Savior, we know our times of prayer are intimate and critical moments. No, we don't "carry" the

---

9   Sheets, D. *Intercessory prayer: How God can use your prayers to move Heaven and Earth*, Ventura, CA: Regal: 1996, 50, 52.

burdens ourselves. We don't "fix" the problems for our loved ones in our own strength. But neither do we forget their needs after praying just once. Petitioning Heaven with persistence is an act of love, not doubt-filled nagging. For some, we continue intercession for years as we meet with God asking for His reconciliation on their behalf.

PRAYING FOR THE HARDENED HEART

I often shake my head wondering why people don't eagerly receive the message of the cross. This sad and weary world desperately needs the Gospel's truth and hope. And yet, people don't readily respond. Like dry, cracked ground, the human heart can harden. Only God knows the intricacies of the barriers in the spiritual realm which prevent individuals from seeing and understanding His plan for redemption in Christ. But through our prayers, fallow ground is plowed up and hearts are softened (Hosea 10:12).

Jesus told the parable of the sower to help his followers understand possible conditions of a hardened heart, making a comparison to soil conditions. Jesus addresses three barriers faced by those who "hear but don't understand": 1) no depth of understanding, 2) a hypocritical spirit, or 3) being distracted by the cares of this world. His use of parables sparked intrigue and got the crowd's attention. Later, the disciples asked Jesus to explain the parable, and doing all He could to deepen the parable's hidden message, Jesus quoted the prophet Isaiah.

> "This is why I speak to them in parables, because seeing they do not see, and hearing they do not hear, nor do they understand. Indeed, in their case the prophecy of Isaiah is fulfilled that says: 'You will indeed hear but never understand, and you will indeed see but never perceive.' For this people›s heart has grown dull, and with their ears they can barely hear, and their eyes they have closed, lest they should see with their eyes and hear with their ears and understand with their heart and turn, and

I would heal them. But blessed are your eyes, for they see, and your ears, for they hear."

Matthew 13:13-16

Verse sixteen of this excerpt addresses the pliable and receptive heart the disciples possessed. But Jesus knew far too many hearts were not receptive to seeds of truth. This resistance hinders spiritual understanding, preventing the veil's removal. Hardened hearts must be softened to become more childlike so the promise of the Gospel message can open eyes to the spiritual realm. Dry, rocky ground is plowed and nourished through prayer. Is it any wonder, then, that our prayers for those who don't yet know Jesus must be persistent?

EMOTIONAL HINDRANCES BECOME STRONGHOLDS

Strangely, the idea of a personal Savior creates a dreaded vulnerability that triggers fear and resistance. Some avoid coming to Jesus because hurt, anger, or confusion create an emotional hindrance in their soul. They feel incapable of addressing the deep-seated cause of their hesitancy. In the vague recesses of their mind, they fear confronting difficult emotions; and because of this anxiety, they refuse to open their heart. Choosing to live in denial, their spiritual vision remains veiled.

Imagine a thistle left unattended in your garden. As it grows, the ugliness scars a beautiful area of the yard. In attempting to pull out the weed, you discover a root so deep it seems impossible to eliminate. You may even give up the effort, acquiescing to your weakness. So, the thistle remains. Unable to reach the depths of the stubborn root leads you to feel helpless, and eventually you determine the only way to cope is by ignoring that area of the garden.

Similar to the thistle, deep-rooted hurts, sins, and mindsets defy removal. Often these begin as coping behaviors developed to deal with the lasting effects of trauma or abuse. In some cases, enduring life's difficulties causes us to question God, and unbelief takes hold in our minds. Some even fall prey to false ideologies as they attempt to reconcile the hard-to-face areas of life. Sadly, this subconscious burial of anger, hurt, and confusion often manifests in sinful choices.

In defining sin as anything that separates us from God, we realize that addictions, habits, thought patterns, and deviant behaviors all fit into the category. We who minister with unveiled face never stand in judgement of others, but neither do we hide the fact that iniquity can harden a heart to the extent that a person feels incapable of overcoming the pattern. Like the gardener choosing to ignore ugly thistles in their yard, parts of the inner man are left buried, unattended and ignored.

CONFRONTING STRONGHOLDS

Consciously or subconsciously, suppressing emotions can bring a false sense of control. The thought patterns justifying denial lead to unbelief. When a person chooses to cope with pain or trauma in these ways, their resistance needs to be addressed lovingly and prayerfully in order to help them face what they cannot face alone.

As believers, we know that Christ's unveiled presence showers the soul with grace, mercy, and deliverance to heal what's been hardened and/or wounded. But how do we impart truth and freedom to those who resist? The answer lies in the principles of ministry already presented in this book: sharing words of truth, acting in compassion, and persevering in prayer. As ministers of the unveiled face, we trust the barrier can be broken through our faithful witness and God's relentless compassion.

Elevating the need for an unveiling, Dutch Sheets references 2 Corinthians 4:3-4:

> "And even if our gospel is veiled, it is veiled to those who are perishing. In their case the god of this world (the devil) has blinded the minds of the unbelievers, to keep them from seeing the light of the gospel of the glory of Christ, who is the image of God."

Hardened hearts prevent a humble response to God's goodness because a veil blinds the spiritual sight of those who don't believe. Sheets likens the veil to a shutter on a photographer's lens.

> The shutter on a camera opens, letting in the light, {and} brings an image. If the shutter on the camera does not open, there will be no image or picture, regardless of how beautiful the scenery or elaborate the setting. The same is true in the souls of human beings ... It makes no difference how glorious our Jesus or wonderful our message, if the veil (shutter) is not removed, there will be no true image (picture) of Christ.[10]

According to Sheets, divine revelation is the necessary ingredient to remove the veil, and illumination only comes through prayer. Sheets equates true repentance to enlightenment (see "A Note About Repentance," Appendix B, page 103). Referencing the Greek word for repentance (*metanoia*), he explains it as a new knowledge—a change of mind.

> In biblical contexts repentance is a new understanding that comes from God through an unveiling (revelation). It is the reversing of the effects of the fall through Adam. Humanity chose their own wisdom, their own knowledge of good and evil, right or wrong. Humanity now needs a new knowledge—from God. Paul said in Acts 26:18 he was called to 'open their eyes'— enlightenment, unveiling, revelation, repentance—so that they may 'turn from darkness to light.'"[11]

PERSEVERE IN PRAYER

Dutch Sheets addresses seven principles of praying for unbelievers. (Note: in the excerpt, Sheets is referring to a man named Kevin as an example of how he applied the points of intercession).

---

10 Sheets, D. *Intercessory prayer: How God can use your prayers to move Heaven and Earth*, Ventura, CA: Regal, 1996, 162.
11 Ibid, 163.

" . . . I taught these principles about praying for the lost . . .

- That God would lift the veil over him (revelation and enlightenment)
- For the Holy Spirit to hover over him and protect him
- For godly people to be in his pathway each day
- To cast down anything that would exalt itself against the knowledge of God, specifically pride and rebellion . . .
- To take down all known strongholds—thought patterns, opinions on religion, materialism, fear . . .
- To bind Satan from taking Kevin captive; to bind all wicked thoughts and lies Satan would try to place in Kevin's mind . . .
- That the armor of God would be placed on him."[12]

Sheets reminds us that persistent prayer is powerful in removing the veil that hinders spiritual sight of those who cannot face their inner strongholds.

> "The unbeliever cannot war for himself. He cannot and will not overcome the strongholds of darkness, and he will not understand the gospel until the veil lifts. We must take our divinely dynamic weapons and fight."[13]

JESUS UNDERSTANDS OUR HUMAN EXPERIENCE

It may be difficult to envision the power emotional hindrances have in the unbeliever's heart and mind. But even Christians can feel incapable of confronting certain places in our souls in our own strength. We, too, resist the healing of wounds and the conviction to change mindsets. Our human nature holds on tightly to its coping behaviors.

When we yield to the strength of our shepherd, however, we realize that Jesus holds and protects us through every step of healing. When we embrace the knowledge that Jesus is our high priest who endured (and understands)

---

12   Ibid, 176.
13   Ibid, 177.

the human condition, we realize He helps us in our weakness. Though Jesus rose above the temptation to deny and bury pain and anger, He understands the struggle. Therefore, He is able to confront brokenness and sin. HE IS ABLE! He takes us by the hand to impart the courage needed to let Him heal the buried places of our souls.

When I become frustrated by God's timing in softening the hardened heart of a person I'm interceding for, I remind myself that if God was able to soften *my* heart, He is more than able to soften the heart of those for whom I pray.

PRAYING IN FAITH

As the book of James exhorts us, we pray in faith, believing God will accomplish what we ask.

> "Therefore, confess your sins to one another and pray for one another, that you may be healed. The prayer of a righteous person has great power as it is working."

James 5:16

We know God hears every prayer, but having the confident assurance God will answer builds our faith. If we doubt we are heard, James tells us we will be like a wave of the sea driven and tossed by the wind (James 1:6). Faith can be built by visualizing meeting with Christ in Heaven, taking the place of access He has granted us. Belief is strengthened when we see ourselves before His throne, laying our loved ones at His feet.

Because prayer is so integral to walking out the ministry of the unveiled face, we come to Jesus in prayer before, during, and after the interactions with others as God ordains and orchestrates. It should be as natural as breathing. Oswald Chambers addresses the honor of praying for others in our everyday encounters.

God brings you to places, among people, and into certain conditions to accomplish a definite purpose through the intercession of the Spirit in you . . . Your part in intercessory prayer is not to agonize over how to intercede, but to use the everyday circumstances and people God puts around you by His providence to bring them before His throne, and to allow the Spirit in you the opportunity to intercede for them.[14]

I encourage you to embrace this role of prayer as a time of precious and cherished fellowship with Christ Jesus, who is always faithful to guide the words we use and to hear the longings of our heart. As Jack Hayford explains, "Prayer is essentially a partnership of the redeemed child of God working hand in hand with God toward the realization of His redemptive purposes on earth."[15]

Each chapter in this book ends with a prayer. These prayers are mere samples anchored in scriptural promises. You should choose your own words to converse with Father God, but realize prayer is a foundational tool for all ministry. Like the mysteries of transmitting electricity, prayer is an unfathomable power that transforms hearts and minds.

Patrick Johnstone (founder of Operation World) writes,

The ministry of the children of God is not doing, but praying, not strategizing, but prostrate before God seeking His will, not clever strategies for manipulating people and events, but trusting in God who moves in the hearts of even His most implacable enemies. Through prayer, Nebuchadnezzar and today's dictators get converted, Manassehs and today's persecutors repent and kingdoms of Babylon and Iron Curtains are torn down. We do

---

14   Chambers, O. *The Golden book of Oswald Chambers: My Utmost for His highest; selections for the year, The Undetected Sacredness of Circumstances*, New York: Dodd, Mead & Company, 1935.

15   Jack W. Hayford, *Prayer Is Invading the Impossible*, South Plainfield, N.J.: Logos International, 1977, revised edition, Bridge Publishing, 1995, 92.

not engage in ministry and pray for God's blessing on it, prayer IS the ministry from which all other ministries must flow.[16]

DON'T GROW WEARY

I can name several close friends on my personal prayer list who seem to have hardened and/or resistant hearts. Their names are written throughout the margins of my journal as I continue to intercede for them. Many are self-reliant, intelligent, and very capable individuals, believing that human reasoning is sufficient for the challenges of life. Others have embraced ideologies in opposition to a personal salvation. Some seem to live in denial, taking on a fatalistic philosophy (e.g. whatever is going to happen is simply fate, and there's nothing they can do about it). Despite my own feelings of inadequacy in addressing their mindset, I continue to pray for opportunities to share. To date, only a few cracks in the door have opened. At times, I get discouraged and I long for the unveiling of Christ's goodness to be made known. But I don't lose heart. Like the widow reminding the judge in Luke 18, I keep asking for their hearts to soften and for revelation to come.

Below is a prayer I regularly pray for these souls. It incorporates Dutch Sheets' principles of prayer for the lost (listed above). I invite you to pray it over those in your life with hardened and resistant hearts.

PRAYER

Jesus, I bring _____ before Your throne, asking for truth to confront denial and deception, and for grace to soften his/her hardened heart. Bring revelation and enlightenment to remove the veil that shields Your goodness, Lord. I ask for Holy Spirit to hover over and protect _____, bringing conviction and humility. I pray for godly people to be placed in his/her path each day. In Your name and by Your blood, I bind

---

16 Johnstone, P. (2020). *Prayer and the Nations.* Accessed October 06, 2020, from https://www.operationworld.org/prayer-and-nations.

ideologies and beliefs that would exalt themselves against the knowledge of God. On their behalf, I bind ungodly thoughts, mindsets, and false imaginations. Specifically, I come against pride and rebellion, asking for the forces of Heaven to break these strongholds. I place a guard around his/her thoughts to prevent temptation. Don't let him/her fall prey to sinful ways of coping. Come alongside him/her to open _____'s ears and eyes to Your truth. Place Your armor on _____ and release revelation and enlightenment. Where repentance is needed, guide him/her to that vulnerable place and help _____ to accept Your loving strength to confront unbelief and sinful habits. Bless him/her with a sorrow that produces repentance without regret. Where there are emotional wounds, hold _____ tightly in Your loving arms and breathe healing to the guarded areas of his/her soul. Bless Your good and perfect work, Jesus, and bring _____ to the realm of glory that lies behind the veil. In Your name I pray. Amen.

REFLECTIONS ON
CHAPTER SEVEN

1. Are you able to envision yourself seated with Christ in the heavens as Hebrews 1:3 describes? If so, describe how this helps you intercede for others. Or tell why you struggle to visualize this image:_____

_____

_____

_____

2. Why is persistence in prayer so important? What strategies might help you be more persistent in your intercession for others?_____

_____

_____

_____

3. After reading the excerpt on repentance in Appendix B, explain any new insights you have about repentance: _____

_____

_____

_____

4. Setting judgment and human analysis aside, list the names of loved ones who seem hardened to receiving Christ. Pray the prayer above over each one, calling their names out to Jesus. Commit to praying for one of these individuals each day (persevering prayer).

_____

_____

_____

As this study concludes and you read the last chapter, prayerfully come before God, asking Him to equip and encourage you to daily walk in the ministry of the unveiled face.

CHAPTER EIGHT

A CALL TO THE MINISTRY OF THE UNVEILED FACE

" . . . I am sending you to open their eyes, so that they may turn from
darkness to light and from the power of Satan to God, that they may receive
forgiveness of sins and a place among those who are sanctified by faith in me."

Acts 26:17-18

Returning to the analogy of a traditional wedding ceremony, God compares the sacrament of marriage to Christ's relationship with His church, reminding us the bridegroom passionately cares for those who yield their lives to Him. Throughout the wedding ceremony a veil shields the bride's beauty until the time comes for it to be uncovered. But as the metaphor applies to life in God's kingdom, the veil actually shields the beauty and goodness of our intended bridegroom, Christ Jesus.

Until the veil is removed, Satan continually works to keep people from encountering the unseen areas of God's kingdom. The evil one aims to deceive, tempting souls to look only at temporary circumstances, interpreting them through limited and fallible human understanding. With this hindered view, we are susceptible to embracing false beliefs. At the moment of salvation, however, the veil is removed so we might gaze upon the full glory of our bridegroom. A transformative love relationship ensues with immediate and eternal blessings.

GOD'S SOVEREIGN ORCHESTRATION

When I reflect on how God orchestrated events leading up to my salvation, I am in awe of what a loving and powerful Lord we serve. Like a masterpiece of art weaves color and light into clarity, the people and resources He provided presented themselves in a symbiotic dance.

One resource God used was the David Wilkerson book, *The Cross and the Switchblade*, which I read at thirteen. After reading the story of how God birthed this ministry to gang members, I strongly felt the call to serve. One afternoon while riding in the back seat of our family car, I had a vision. I saw myself at a type of snack stand where people would come and I would serve the refreshment they hungered for. The vision was brief and had little detail, but it has stuck with me. To date, I've never opened a stand from which to serve, but I do know the call to minister to those He brings my way is upon me, as it is upon us all.

We may wish the call were more defined and we knew the specifics of what to do. But because our prayers are heard, we need not worry about the organized logistics of ministry. Though there will be plenty of moments when God provides explicit guidance, yielding to the vagueness of the call becomes a sweet reliance on His sovereignty. God knows each step of the process, and the Holy Spirit serves as our faithful guide. No move has to be taken in our own strength, and going step-by-step ensures we are listening for His voice.

The ministry of the unveiled face is a ministry of opportunity and obedience, ignited by prayers of intercession and beautifully wrapped in acts of compassion and words of truth. Just as God orchestrated the events leading to my personal salvation, He does so for everyone. Like a masterful conductor of a harmonious orchestra, He directs us to play our part as we follow His leading. Each of us plays an integral role in what God orchestrates for others in the grand design of His symphony. We simply produce music according to the cue of His baton, so we are always prayerfully looking for opportunities He brings our way in life's ordinary moments.

NOT A RANDOM OR HAPHAZARD DESIGN

Let there be no confusion, however. The ministry of the unveiled face should not be interpreted as random or disorganized. God has a definite plan and purpose for all believers. Perhaps some have a more distinct call than others. But nothing in God's kingdom is haphazard. He is in charge, not us! The enormity of the work of God's kingdom is difficult to fathom and can be overwhelming. God has tightened every bolt and secured every beam. Our role is simply faithful obedience and trust in our bridegroom. We are not on a wayward path. God provides rudders to keep our vessel sailing in the right direction.

In 1 Corinthians 12, Paul talks about the body of Christ being comprised of many parts, emphasizing the important function of each. Earlier in 1 Corinthians, Paul addresses the distinction between his role and the role of another apostle, Apollos, when he talks about one planting the seeds and the other watering (1 Corinthians 3:4-9). He emphasizes God alone as the source of growth. Paul and Apollos were each doing their part to facilitate the growth. Like them, we find our anchor in trusting the "whole" of God's work, not fretting over our specific task(s).

The ministry of the unveiled face is about planting and watering seeds as God directs. It is also about grounding ourselves in prayer, asking for truth and light to take deep root in nourished soil. But it is God who causes the growth. In reaching out to those Christ serendipitously brings our way, we don't need to understand fully where He is leading. We simply obey His voice, responding to everyday, God-ordained opportunities.

According to Oswald Chambers, this means we are God's very special choice, available to minister in the apparent random surroundings He has engineered.

Yet we never realize that all the time God is at work in our everyday events and in the people around us. If we will only obey, and do the task that He has placed closest to us, we will see Him. One of the most amazing revelations of God comes to us when we learn that it is in the everyday things of life that we realize the magnificent deity of Jesus Christ."[17]

OPENING BLIND EYES

In Paul's letter to the Romans, he tells us God's invisible qualities and divine nature are evident within the minds of the people in the natural world through His creation. But by choosing sin and unbelief they refuse to honor Him, so their foolish hearts become darkened (Romans 1:19-21). Paul exhorts us to pray their eyes will be opened to that evidence and their minds will receive the hidden treasure of truth.

The ministry of the unveiled face opens eyes to reconciliation with God. We know in Christ, God reconciles the world to Himself, so our sins might not be counted against us (1 Corinthians 5:16-20). As ambassadors, we know Christ lives in us for that same purpose: to reconcile the souls of humankind to their Creator. The old is gone and the new has come. We speak and pray transformative words of truth into people's lives as we naturally interact with them in everyday places and circumstances. God's light then pierces through to the darkest areas of their soul.

On the night of the Last Supper, Jesus told His disciples, "You did not choose me, but I chose you and appointed you to go and bear fruit" (John 15:16). This spiritual fruit ripens by our reflecting Christ to others, as in a mirror, so the power of truth illuminates revelation and insight. We are the bridegroom's friends, after all, and our sincerest hope is to invite others to the wedding feast.

---

17 Chambers, O. *The Golden book of Oswald Chambers: My Utmost for His highest; selections for the year, Spiritual Dejection.* New York: Dodd, Mead & Company, 1935.

May the prayers offered in this book provide you with a foundation from which to build as you intercede for others. And may the following prayer I specifically pray for you equip you for this ministry and the hope of your calling.

PRAYER (BASED ON EPHESIANS 1)

Almighty God, I give thanks for all who read this book, and I humbly ask Your blessing of grace and strength to be with them. Equip them, O God, for the work You have called them to as they love and serve others in Your name. Impart words of truth to speak and pray so powers of darkness will be bound and the light of Christ will be revealed. Remove the veil of deception shrouding the spiritual vision and understanding of those they interact with. By the power of the Holy Spirit, make the radiance of Your goodness known. And now, Lord God, grant them the spirit of wisdom and revelation in the knowledge of You, and may the eyes of their understanding be enlightened that they may know the hope of their calling, the riches of the glory of their inheritance, and the exceeding greatness of Your power. In Christ's name I pray. Amen.

REFLECTIONS ON CHAPTER EIGHT (AND THE ENTIRE STUDY)

1. Throughout this book are many metaphors. Metaphors deepen understanding by comparing something intangible to something tangible (Jesus used them all the time in parables). Below are metaphors from this study. Choose a few that really speak to you and commit to internalizing them so you might carry these principles of ministry with you as you interact with others. Jot down your thoughts about how the metaphor resonates with you.

a. Comparing a personal relationship with Christ to that of a bride and bridegroom (Chapter One):

_____

_____

_____

b. Comparing the veil that hinders spiritual understanding to the veil of a bride (Chapter One):

_____

_____

_____

c. Comparing the fragrance of Christ in us to a peaceful flower garden intricately patterned (Chapter Three):_____

_____

_____

_____

d. Comparing the word of God to a sharp sword (biblical metaphor referenced in Chapter Four): _____

_____

_____

_____

e. Comparing our reflection of Christ to how the moon reflects the sun (Chapter Six): _____

_____

_____

_____

f. Comparing the promises and assurances of God to an enormous and bottomless treasure chest (Chapter Six): _____

_____

_____

_____

g. Comparing hardened hearts to dry, cracked ground (Chapter Seven):

_____

_____

_____

_____

h. Comparing emotional strongholds to an ugly thistle growing in a garden (Chapter Seven): _____

_____

_____

_____

i. Comparing the veil that shields understanding to the shutter on a camera lens (Dutch Sheet's metaphor in Chapter Seven): _____

_____

_____

_____

j. Comparing the enlightenment of repentance to a campfire lighting up the dark night sky (Appendix B): _____

_____

_____

_____

k. Comparing the ministry of the unveiled face to an orchestra where God is the conductor and we are the instrumentalists (Chapter Eight):

_____

_____

_____

l. Comparing God-ordained ministry to a masterpiece of art weaving color and light into clarity (Chapter Eight): _____

_____

_____

_____

2. To help retain what you've learned from this study, list several "takeaways" you want to remember. If helpful, take time to re-read your highlights and underlines.

_____

_____

_____

3. Are there lingering questions or wonderings you have about the ministry of the unveiled face? If so, list those here:

_____

_____

_____

A NOTE ABOUT UNBELIEF

The popular belief that the energy of the universe can be equated with God is a dangerous line of thinking. Satan uses this ideology to foster unbelief. The vagueness of the philosophy is appealing since it limits faith to a simple acknowledgement that God exists "out there, somewhere" in the collective energy of the cosmos. But that undefined description of the Creator is basically an expression of doubt and avoidance. Once that ambiguous line of thinking takes root, the heart hardens to the truth of God's design and the power of His promises.

The book of Hebrews warns against a spirit of unbelief, pointing out a hardened heart cannot enter God's rest (Hebrews 3:12-13). As we consider the invisible veil preventing spiritual wisdom and understanding, we realize it is a cloud of deception leading to unbelief. Clouds shield light, hindering accurate vision. As Hebrews 11 tells us, it is faith that brings the assurance of God's supernatural transcendence to our natural realm as the only hope for humanity (Hebrews 11:1-3).

When we pray for others, we should pray they receive words of truth united in faith, so the power of God's promises will take root in their souls. Faith obliterates doubt and unbelief, bringing a powerful rest to the weary soul (Hebrews 4:2). Asking God to increase the measure of faith plows up the fallow ground of a hardened heart (Hosea 10:12). Words of truth impart hope drawing the unbeliever to the realm of God's goodness behind the veil.

A NOTE ABOUT REPENTANCE

Repentance is a prerequisite for salvation. Some may feel this is a harsh demand, but that line of thinking suggests a misunderstanding. Paul tells us the Lord's kindness leads to repentance (Romans 2:4), so we know the call to turn to Jesus is all about laying down what is not His best for us. Repentance removes the veil that shields God's goodness. But the vulnerability required for repentance is also enhanced by knowing just how good God is. Like a campfire lights up the beauty of a dark and remote mountain wilderness, repentance awakens light and glory in every darkened place.

The Old Testament story of Job culminates in the moment Job finally grasps God's sovereignty. Job cries out to God for understanding, and God answers by revealing how much Job does not know (Job 38 and 39). God makes known the works of His creation with an unfathomable list of what was accomplished at the beginning of time. "Where were you when I laid the foundations of the earth? Tell me if you have understanding" (Job 38:4). In a broken response to this enlightenment, Job humbly repents, admitting his limited assumptions about God. Realizing that God is so much bigger than what he once believed, Job cries out, "I have heard of you by the hearing of the ear; But now my eye sees You; therefore I retract, And I repent in dust and ashes" (Job 42:5-6). Job's new knowledge of God's sovereignty brought revelation, repentance, and the understanding he desperately sought.

The call to repentance is not a condition of a harsh God, but rather a beckoning from a God who lovingly finds a way to remove the veil that keeps souls in dark places. Repentance is hastened by an enlightened awakening of God's goodness. It is liberating to change our view of it from a conditional REQUIREMENT we must strive for, to an awestruck RESPONSE to God's sovereign kindness.

BIBLIOGRAPHY

Bounds, E. M. *The Complete Works of E.M. Bounds on Prayer*. Grand Rapids, MI: Baker Book House, 1990.

Chambers, O. *The Golden book of Oswald Chambers: My Utmost for His highest; selections for the year*. New York: Dodd, Mead & Company, 1935.

Ciano, Rachel, "Luther's Doctrine of the Priesthood of All Believers: The Importance for Today," *Credo Magazine*, Jan. 8, 2020. https://credomag.com/2020/01/luthers-doctrine-of-the-priesthood-of-all-believers-the-importance-for-today.

Etheridge, Kristy, "Inside a BGEA Crusade: Prayer, Preparation and More Prayer," Jan. 7, 2014, accessed Feb. 2, 2021. https://billygraham.org/story/inside-a-bgea-crusade-prayer-preparation-and-more-prayer.

"Billy Graham's Life and Ministry by the numbers," (Feb 21, 2018), *Lifeway Research*, Feb. 2, 2021. https://lifewayresearch.com/2018/02/21/billy-grahams-life-ministry-by-the-numbers.

Hayford, Jack W. *Prayer Is Invading the Impossible*. South Plainfield, N.J.: Logos International, 1977; revised edition, Bridge Publishing, 1995.

Johnstone, P. *Prayer and the Nations*. 2020, accessed October 06, 2020, https://www.operationworld.org/prayer-and-nations.

Sheets, D. Intercessory Prayer: How God can use your prayers to move Heaven and Earth. Ventura, CA: Regal, 1996.

Smith, Gregory A., Alan Cooperman, Besheer Mohamed, Elizabeth Podrebarac Sciupac, Becka A. Alper, Kiana Cox, and Claire Gecewicz. "In U.S., Decline of Christianity Continues at Rapid Pace." *Pew Research Center*, (October 17, 2019), accessed January 23, 2021. https://www.pewforum. org/2019/10/17/in-u-s-decline-of-christianity-continues-at-rapid-pace.

Spurgeon, Charles H. "A View of God's Glory," a sermon by C.H. Spurgeon, The Spurgeon Archive, Collection administered by Midwestern Baptist Theological Seminary. Hosted by WP Engine, 1908. https://archive. spurgeon.org/sermons/3120.php

For more information about
Janet E. Fichter
and

The Ministry of the Unveiled Face
please visit:

www.atjesusfeet.com

Janet is available to provide guidance to any individual or small
group utilizing this book as a tool for study or discussion.

For more information about
AMBASSADOR INTERNATIONAL
please visit:

www.ambassador-international.com
@AmbassadorIntl
www.facebook.com/AmbassadorIntl

Thank you for reading this book. Please consider leaving us a
review on your social media, favorite retailer's website,
Goodreads or Bookbub, or our website.

Display OF HIS Splendor

Stepping Out to Meet
the Needs of Our Generation

AMILLIAH KENYA

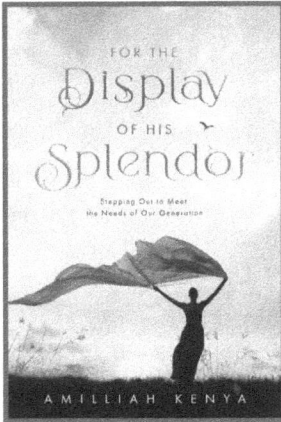

Is your heart touched by the emotional distress, mental illness, hopelessness, despair, addiction, fear, anxiety, uncertainty, and fatigue that characterizes our day? Within the foundations of despair and hopelessness is the cry, "Can someone help me? Can someone call on God for me?" God is not deaf to the cries of this generation—He created you with this generation in mind. He has equipped you for the difficult times ahead. Allow God to guide and to work through you. Display His splendor to those around you.

This book is not a self-help book filled with platitudes from people who think they have life figured out. Instead, Marilyn Nutter and April White link arms with the audience and encourage their readers through stories of their personal challenges in widowhood and chronic illness. Women are encouraged to see loss and hardship as part of life's journey and are reminded to turn their gaze upwards, to the Provider of Hope.

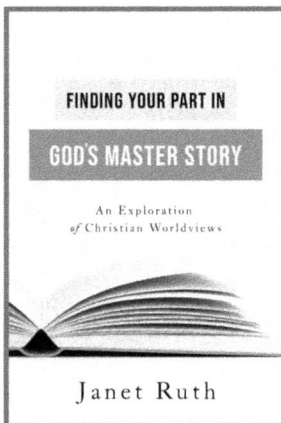

MARILYN NUTTER and APRIL WHITE

DESTINATION HOPE

a travel companion when
life falls apart

FINDING YOUR PART IN

GOD'S MASTER STORY

An Exploration
of Christian Worldviews

Janet Ruth

Whether we realize it or not, we all have an internal belief system—a worldview—which directs our thoughts and actions. Our worldview is how we understand the world around us—where we came from, how we should live, and what our purpose is. Examining your personal worldview in light of God's Master Story can strengthen your faith and clarify your purpose in this world.

www.ingramcontent.com/pod-product-compliance
Lightning Source LLC
Chambersburg PA
CBHW071454070426
42452CB00039B/1357